Seeking a State of Heaven

This book is dedicated to all the people who have visited, or are yet to visit, the city of Haifa in Israel, who would like to know who the German Templers were, and what inspired them to build their beautiful colony at the base of Mount Carmel.

SEEKING A STATE OF HEAVEN

The German Templers

*Their beliefs, their mission and their connection
with the Bahá'ís in Haifa*

Carolyn Sparey Fox

GR

GEORGE RONALD
OXFORD

George Ronald, Publisher
Oxford
www.grbooks.com

A catalogue record for this book is available from the British Library

ISBN 978-0-85398-613-3

Cover design: René Steiner, Steinergraphics.com

Contents

Acknowledgements

I would like to thank Dr Julia Martin of the Temple Society for permission to quote passages from *Jerusalem Journey* by Christopher Hoffmann, translated into English and abridged by Gertrude Paulus. Also, Stephen N. Lambden for permission to use his translation of Bahá'u'lláh's Tablet to Georg David Hardegg and for writing a short commentary to be included in the book. Thanks, too, to my husband Jeremy Fox for his encouragement and for providing a further short commentary on Bahá'u'lláh's Tablet to Hardegg.

It goes without saying that without the publisher, George Ronald, the unfolding story of the German Templers may have remained a long-forgotten history, and I thank my editor, May Hofman, for her patience and attention to detail in the process of bringing the Templer story to the modern reader.

Prologue

On 30 October 1868, Christoph Hoffmann and Georg David Hardegg arrived with their families by steamer at the Port of Haifa, in Palestine; they had journeyed by land and sea all the way from the German State of Württemberg, and whilst their arrival on the shores of the Holy Land marked the end of a long journey, it was also the beginning of a venture for which they had spent years preparing, for they were German Templers, and they were on their way to set up a small colony in Nazareth, about 25 miles inland. However, destiny had other plans, and following the advice of the Prussian Consul in Beirut and a trusted young Christian missionary, James J. Huber, who was living in Nazareth, they were persuaded to abandon their original destination and settle in the vicinity of Haifa, where postal connections, travel and the promise of good land for agriculture were more than enough to tempt them.

Two months earlier, on the morning of 31 August, another group had arrived at the Port of Haifa by steamer, their final destination being the prison city of Akka, which lay a few miles away at the northern end of Haifa bay. Unlike the German Templers, this earlier group were exiles at the mercy of the Ottoman Empire, their arrival in Palestine marking their fourth and final destination following 15 years of successive banishments from Persia. Their leader, Bahá'u'lláh, was the founder of the latest of the world's major religions, the Bahá'í Faith, and those who shared his banishment were members of His family and a number of His followers.

Although there was no apparent connection between these two groups of people arriving in Haifa during the latter half of 1868, the relationship which they established within just a couple of years, despite difficulties of language, suggested that they had more in common than the Templers could ever have imagined. And so the questions arise:

Who, exactly, were the German Templers, and why did their Christian belief inspire them to leave their German homes in order to build a community in Palestine?

Who were the Bahá'ís, what did they believe, and why had they been banished to the prison city of Akka in Palestine?

And what connection, if any, could there possibly be between two such diverse groups from such different cultures, one from the east and the other from the west?

The German Templers were undoubtedly influenced, as were all Christians at the time, by the eventful and somewhat chequered Christian history which preceded them, and although Christian history per se isn't the subject of this book, the Introduction offers a brief overview in order to establish exactly how and why Templer doctrine originated and to help put their story into a wider context. In the process of unfolding this story and in the light of what took place preceding it, we are also in a position to shed light on the Mission of Bahá'u'lláh, for as the book moves forward it will be seen that the two appear to be inextricably linked. Bahá'u'lláh's appearance during the mid-19th century fulfilled the promises and prophecies not only of the Old and New Testaments in relation to the Second Coming of Christ, but also the promises contained in all the major religions of the world.

Introduction

A Brief Overview of Christianity in the West

. . . be not conformed to this world: but be ye transformed by the renewing of your mind, that ye may prove what is that good, and acceptable, and perfect, will of God.
Romans 12:2

The story of Jesus Christ, his message, and the early history of Christianity are all told in the New Testament of the Bible, and although there are anomalies, it nevertheless offers a rich and beautiful insight to what Jesus taught and how the first Christians spread his teachings beyond the part of the world in which they lived. However, the New Testament only came into existence as a book towards the end of the fourth century, the Roman Church not only preventing their Christian flock from having access to it, but also prohibiting any translation from the Latin into another language, with the result that the Christian population had to rely on the clergy for their Christian guidance and inspiration. Thus they were denied the possibility of having first-hand knowledge of the story of Jesus as written in the four Gospels, or of the first extraordinary Christian teachers in the Acts of the Apostles and the Epistles, and the prophetic vision of the future set out in the Revelation of St John.

Christian history is a patchwork of different interpretations, violent disagreements, turmoil and war, and through all the numerous attempts to gain enlightenment and the ultimate truth of Christ's teachings, certain basic tenets invariably reappeared from age to age, one of which is relevant to the subject of this book; it involves the coming of the Kingdom of God on earth and the return of Christ, and down the centuries it has been something preoccupying certain deep-thinking Christians with access to the Bible as they pondered Biblical prophecy and Christ's own promises for future times.

During the first and second centuries following the birth of Christianity belief in Christ's return was an integral part of the Christian Faith, a doctrine which the Greek theologian, Origen, changed during the first half of the third century, when he stated that the return of Christ was spiritual in nature.[1] The 19th century English poet and theologian Samuel Taylor Coleridge wrote of this change in doctrine: 'the pastors of the church had gradually changed the light and life of the Gospel into the very superstitions they were commissioned to disperse, and thus paganised Christianity in order to christen paganism'.[2] Despite the strict ruling on the subject by the Catholic Church, there were many Christians over the following centuries who defied it, who chose to believe what was written in the Scriptures, and who were more often than not labelled as heretics.

In 16th century Western Europe the powerful control with which the Roman Catholic Church had held Christian believers in a state of submission for over 1,000 years was monumentally challenged. Although Christians had sought answers to deep theological questions of faith since Christianity was born at the start of the first century A.D., the challenge which emerged during the 16th century was a catalyst for a virtual Pandora's box in Christian thinking and belief over the centuries to come.

A key point of contention was the Holy Bible to which most Christians had no access since it was written in a language which they couldn't understand; this suited the Pope and the clergy, who believed that they, and they alone, were authorized to guide and teach the Christian community. There were, however, some enlightened theologians who believed that many of these official teachings were contrary to those set out in the Bible. A leading light in the quest for change had emerged in England during the 14th century in the person of John Wycliffe, who was a theologian, philosopher, and professor at Oxford University, and who bravely translated the Bible into Middle English. Many years after his death the current Pope rewarded Wycliffe's dedicated work by digging up his remains and having them crushed and thrown in the river.

John Wycliffe was also of the opinion that the end of the world was close, an opinion which he shared in his treatise of 1356 entitled *The Last Age of the Church*. His 19th-century biographer, Thomas Murray, wrote that

> his imagination being struck, and his heart affected with the alarming event which was passing before his eyes, he imbibed the unfounded opinion, that the day of judgement was at hand, and that the close of the 14th century would be the end of the world. An opinion somewhat similar had been entertained by many eminent writers before the time of Wycliff; and therefore our reformer was only indulging in speculations which had obtained the sanction of the greatest names.[3]

John Wycliffe's influence was widespread, his writings inspiring theologians and philosophers as far as South Bohemia, where the priest Jan Hus (1369–1415) was burned at the stake for his work towards church reform more than a century before Martin Luther made his mark in establishing the Protestant Reformation in Germany; some sources claim that copies of Wycliffe's manuscript Bibles were used as kindling for the fire. As far as Martin Luther's contribution to reform was concerned, it was thanks to the recent invention of the printing press that within two months of writing his famous 'Ninety-Five Theses' in October 1517 he was able to spread his ideas beyond the university of Wittenberg, where he was professor of theology, and into the far corners of Europe.[4] As a result of his blatant refusal to retract his ideas, Luther was excommunicated from the church, condemned as a heretic and forced to escape to Warburg Castle, close to the town of Eisenach. It was here that, in keeping with his firm belief that all Christians should have access to reading the Bible, he began translating it into German,[5] using a 1516 Greek translation of the New Testament by Desiderius Erasmus, (1466–1436) a Dutch priest who was recognized as being one of the greatest scholars of the northern Renaissance.

It is interesting to note that apart from his quest for church reform, Luther was also clearly of the opinion that the return of Christ was very close, and that the end of the world was imminent. Indeed, as he began translating the Old Testament he decided to tackle the prophetic Book of Daniel first, for the edification of Christians living in what he sincerely believed to be the last days of the world. Luther was reported to have spoken and written of the end times on several occasions, variously stating that the end would take place by the year 1548, or before a hundred years were up, or that the world couldn't last for another 300 years, i.e. beyond the mid-1800s.

There's no doubt that Martin Luther was one of the most influential figures in the reform movement, but there were also other notable advocates for major reform who are closely associated with the Protestant Reformation, although they weren't all necessarily in agreement regarding what reforms were needed or exactly how far they should go. The Swiss priest and theologian, Ulrich Zwingli, born in 1484, was of the opinion that Luther's ideas didn't go far enough, and whereas Luther, who was largely driven by a fear of hell and of God, had a preoccupation with saving his own soul, Zwingli, who had a passion and love for his country, was concerned with saving his own people and reforming society; he also became embroiled in the conflict between the Catholic and Protestant Cantons in Switzerland, joining the Zurich army as field chaplain and dying in battle, his body chopped into pieces and burnt to ashes.

Possibly the most influential protagonist heading the Protestant Reformation was John Calvin, who was born in France in

1509, and who was inspired both by Erasmus and by Luther, who was twenty years his senior. It was when Calvin was living in Paris (1533) that he collaborated in the writing of an inflammatory address criticizing traditional theologians and calling the Church to return to the pure ideals of the New Testament; fleeing the uproar which followed, Calvin reportedly jumped from an upper window with the aid of bedsheets, and escaped the city disguised as a farmer, complete with hoe slung over his shoulder. He managed to find refuge in Basel, Switzerland, for a while, and it was here, in the year 1536, that he first published what became his most celebrated book, *Institutes of the Christian Religion*, a guide to understanding the new Evangelical faith. It was during this period that he noted his belief in future events related to the Second Coming of Christ, writing,

> Christ will come, not for the destruction of the world, but for the purposes of salvation. The Scripture uniformly commands us to look forward with eager expectation to the coming of Christ . . . we must hunger after Christ, we must seek, contemplate, etc, till the dawning of that great day when our Lord will fully manifest the glory of his kingdom.[6]

John Calvin eventually settled in Geneva, where he successfully restructured the church, seeking to create a model Christian community in which the church dominated the state and dictated its running according to Christian guidelines. It was a strict regime which people ignored at their peril, and when a member of the city council accused Calvin of preaching false doctrine and refusing, when ordered, to withdraw his statement, he was obliged to walk through the streets wearing only a shirt and carrying a torch. Torture and beheading were the fate of many who dared to disobey Calvin's severe rules.

Nevertheless, John Calvin's influence spread from Switzerland to Hungary, Germany and Scotland, and although the Reformation in England was connected with what was taking place in Europe, it was the English King Henry VIII's desire to divorce his wife – which was against Catholic doctrine – that provided the final break with Rome, Henry establishing himself as Supreme Head of the Church of England. Henry appointed as his chaplain the former Bishop of Worcester, Hugh Latimer, who gives a glimpse of certain Christian thinking at the time in his sermon on the Lord's Prayer, writing of a future parliament, 'a parliament in which Christ shall rule and not men; and which the righteous pray for when they say, "Thy kingdom come," because they know that therein reformation of all things shall be had.'[7]

Latimer was not alone; several fellow bishops and churchmen expressed similar sentiments, and in Scotland, the great reformer John Knox expressed his belief by writing, 'has not the Lord Jesus, in spite of Satan's malice, carried up our flesh into heaven? And should he not return? We know that he shall return, and that with expedition.'[8]

The Reformation changed the face of Christianity throughout Europe, transforming Christian thought and practice, and opening the way to enable Christians to look at their faith in a new light. Martin Luther, Ulrich Zwingli and John Calvin were the leaders of what became labelled as the Magisterial Reformation, so named due to the support it received from the civil authorities (civil magistrates and territorial princes), all of whom no doubt had their own political agendas. However, although many Christians welcomed and embraced change, there were some who believed that reform didn't go far enough. Those in the Christian population wishing to take the whole reform movement a step further became a part of what was known as the Radical Reformation, an umbrella term which included many different radical groups throughout Europe who were strongly against a relationship between church and state, their common belief being that the church should be rebuilt from the grass roots upwards by following the simple teachings of the New Testament. Those adhering to a firm belief that Christian baptism should be administered only to adults were labelled 'Anabaptist',[9] and those practising it were hounded mercilessly by both the Roman Catholic Church and the Magisterial reformers alike for disobeying the strict ruling, their writings often destroyed and their followers facing death by burning or drowning. Although there were numerous issues which the various factions deliberated and argued over, there were many in the Radical Reformation who held a common chiliastic view of future events, involving an expectation of the Second Coming of Christ, the establishment of God's Kingdom on earth, and the imminent end of the world.

Numerous Christian communities were born from the Radical Reformation, including the Mennonites, the Hutterites and the Amish. And human nature being what it is, the quest for the perfect church and the perfect Christian life continued, believers dividing into ever more sects, each sect claiming to have found the ultimate Christianity as revealed in the New Testament. One such movement which originated from within German Lutherism during the 17th century was Pietism, in some ways a product of the devastating Thirty Years War (1618–1648), which had started out as a war between various Protestant (Reformed) and Catholic States and which at its close left much of Central Europe in a state of destruction and chaos. Out of the resulting physical devastation and spiritual malaise came a renewed thirst for spiritual nourishment, and for many Christians seeking enlightenment and inner peace, Pietism offered the solution. Pietism was also the background from which the German Templers emerged, from which they drew their inspiration and formed their own particular doctrines.

1
Light upon Light: Pietism

If therefore thou shalt not watch, I will come on thee as a thief,
and thou shalt not know what hour I will come upon thee.
Revelation 3:3

The new Enlightenment which was Pietism inspired Christians from all backgrounds, eventually covering vast areas not
only of Europe, but also of Russia and America. Pietism was
the root from which the German Templers flowered, influenc-
ing what was to become their own distinctive doctrine which
led to their decision to create a Christian community in the
Holy Land.

The man generally recognized as being the father of Pietism
was Philipp Jacob Spener (1635–1705), a pastor in Frankfurt
who, disturbed both by what he observed to be an absence of
spirituality in the city following the war, and by a rigid Lutheran
orthodoxy lacking personal commitment to the Christian life,
set up meetings in his home for Christian devotion and conversation. No doubt encouraged by the success of this venture,
he then published his statement, 'Pia Desideria' (Holy Desire)[1]
in which he focused particularly on the importance of active
personal faith and good Christian living. Individual spiritual
rebirth in conjunction with an active Christian community
was the core belief of Pietism, added to which, inspired by
passages in the Book of Revelation, a focus on service and
missionary work was seen to be of vital importance in hasten-
ing the return of Christ, something which the more extreme
Pietists anticipated in the not too distant future. Those who
followed this Pietist movement considered it to be an extension of the earlier Reformation, and despite disapproval from
the orthodox Lutherans, they stressed that their teachings were
deeply grounded in those of Martin Luther.

Initially Pietism embraced a wide variety of reformers who corresponded with one another on the best way to improve the existing church. By the late 17th century, however, this had developed into two separate streams of Pietists, one which wished to improve what they viewed as the relatively conservative established church, and the other, known as Radical Pietism, believing that this was impossible, the only way towards renewal being to separate from the established church altogether. However, as with all previous attempts to create the ultimate Christian system, Radical Pietism, too, became a vast patchwork of different groups and societies, some of which throw light on how the Templers evolved their ideas. Despite certain differences in doctrine all Pietist factions did nevertheless share a few core convictions, including the desire for a more heartfelt religion, more participation in church matters from the congregation, the experience of spiritual rebirth, and the use of unofficial religious meetings.

Many Radical Pietists were influenced by the writings of the German Lutheran and mystic, Jakob Böhme (1575–1624), who was a master shoemaker by trade, and who was firmly of the opinion that concepts of God and the Christian life shouldn't depend on certain set and established beliefs; this greatly angered the clergy, who believed that only they had any authority as far as God and Christian living were concerned. Many of Böhme's writings were translated into English, and someone who was greatly attracted to his ideas was an Anglican priest living in England by the name of John Pordage (1607–1681). He in turn influenced Jane Leade (1623–1704), who founded the Philadelphia Society in London in 1694 in order to gather together Christians who had moved away from Catholicism, or what she referred to as 'the Babel of Christendom'.[2]

In Philadelphian thinking, the church of Philadelphia represented the millennial age, specifically in connection with the return of Christ, with some believers expecting that the year 1700 would initiate the first stirrings in preparation for the

arrival of Christ's millennial kingdom on earth.[3] Through translation of Jane Leade's writings into German, her ideas were soon
being widely read on the Continent; of particular note was the
influence her ideas had on one Count Heinrich Albrecht, who
was so affected by the ecstasy experienced by believers during
Easter celebrations in Berleburg Castle in 1700 that he and his
family adopted Philadelphian belief, including its millennial
approach, the fulfilment of which they believed to be imminent.
By the 1730s Berleburg was a thriving centre of the Philadelphian society, which was also spreading into parts of western
Germany and Switzerland; a few decades later the author Jung-
Stilling noted that at no time in the history of the church had
the expectation of Christ's Second Coming been as striking
and universal as it was during the first half of the 18th century.
Indeed, Jung-Stilling's personal interest had far reaching consequences, as will soon be seen.

A notable adherent of Radical Pietism was Nikolaus Ludwig,
Graf (Count) von Zinzendorf (1700–1760), whose maternal
grandmother had been a follower and friend of Philipp Spener,
the father of Pietism. On inheriting part of his grandmother's
land[4] Zinzendorf turned his attention to a group of tenants
who had sought asylum from him, refugees from Bohemia
and Moravia who were adherents of the persecuted Moravian
Brethren[5] and who, in 1722, with his encouragement and
leadership, established a new village, Herrnhut ('The Lord's
Watch') on his estate. One of the rather extraordinary results of
this enterprise was the commencement, in 1727, of a hundred
years of continuous prayer, known as the Hourly Interces-
sion, made by relays of both men and women. Evangelism
and missionary ventures resulted, with missionaries travelling
to Greenland, North America, the West Indies, and England,
where in 1738 Charles and John Wesley formed a deep and
significant relationship with the Moravians.[6]

The other, more conservative arm of Pietism was based in
the State of Württemberg. It was Philipp Spener himself who

introduced the ideas of Pietism into Württemberg when he visited the area in the 1660s. Favourable conditions guaranteed success, not least that there was no opposition from the princes, with positive encouragement coming from church authorities.

One of the most prominent Pietists in the State of Württemberg was Johann Albrecht Bengel, who, due to his influence on Templer theology nearly a hundred years later, deserves more than a passing mention. Bengel was born in 1687 in the town of Winnenden, in the Stuttgart Region of Württemberg. His father, who was a minister in the town, died when Bengel was just six years old, and four months later the family home was destroyed by fire during a French plunder campaign into the Württemberg region. Bengel not only lost his home, but also his father's extensive theological library, something which he later felt to be fortuitous in his personal spiritual journey, in that this tragedy actually took away the temptation to study too many books, leaving him with just the Bible. In 1706 he was ordained as a Lutheran pastor, spending the rest of his life variously teaching, researching, writing, and serving as a church dignitary.

Johann Albrecht Bengel was a great believer in the critical analysis of Biblical text, and was disturbed by the substantial variety of Greek texts available at the time. It was for this reason that in 1734 he decided to create his own edition of the Greek New Testament, offering what he believed to be a definitive and true rendering of God's word. In 1742 he followed this up with an in-depth interpretation of the New Testament (*Gnomon Novi Testamenti*), before launching himself into his own New Testament in German with the purpose of making the word of God accessible to the general population. But Bengel didn't stop there, for as a result of his belief that the Bible offered not only salvation but also an over-arching view of the entire history of humanity from the very beginning to the very end, he set about producing a massive and elaborate chronological system from which he calculated, amongst other things, the year of Christ's return, which is often referred to as the time of the end. When reminded that even Christ himself was unable to give a time for his return, as in Mark 13:32, or in the Acts of the Apostles 1:7,[7] he argued that only after his ascension did Christ become aware of it, revealing it to John in the Book of Revelation. Bengel's meticulous study of history, mathematics and Biblical texts led him to the conclusion that the Second Coming of Jesus Christ would take place in the year 1836, just eight years short of the year 1844 which the 19th-century American Adventist William Miller predicted. Bengel was sure he was correct in his calculations, but in case of failure he hastened to add that should his date pass without a result, then his calculations should be checked for any mistakes. Since he died in 1752, nearly a hundred years earlier than his predicted date, he didn't live long enough to know whether he was right or not, or indeed, to face the consequences of either result.

Amongst Bengel's contemporaries who were influenced by his work was John Wesley, who had already come into contact with Pietist thinking during a voyage across the Atlantic in 1735; he had formed a relationship with the Moravians in 1738, as already mentioned, and not only studied Bengel's commentary on the Book of Revelation, but also made use of his interpretation of the New Testament (*Gnomon Novi Testamenti*). Also influenced by Bengel was the famous watchmaker, inventor and theologian Philipp Matthaus Hahn who, no doubt inspired by Bengel's intricate chronological system, went so far as to construct an astronomical clock using Bengel's eschatological calculations. Hahn's daughter, Beate, was later to become closely connected with the German Templers, not only through her sons' involvement but also through her daughter, who was to marry Christoph Hoffmann, the founder of the movement. Yet another contemporary who drew inspiration from Bengel was previously mentioned author Johann Heinrich Jung-Stilling, an extraordinary man who towards

Johann Heinrich Jung-Stilling

the end of his life inadvertently caused the mass migration of Pietist Christians into southern Russia in search of what was, in effect, the New Jerusalem.[8] And it is to Johann Heinrich Jung-Stilling that we turn in the next chapter.

2

'Longing for Heaven':
Johann Heinrich Jung-Stilling

*For as the lightning cometh out of the east, and shineth even unto
the west;
so shall also the coming of the Son of man be.*
Matt. 24: 27

Born in Germany in 1740, Jung-Stilling had ambitions above
and beyond his trade as a tailor, and at the age of 15, with the
help and encouragement of a local clergyman, he was able to
acquire a teaching position in a local hamlet, commenting in
his memoir that his 'method of teaching was peculiar . . .';[1]
unfortunately he neglected to explain what this peculiar aspect
of his teaching method referred to! What excited him more
than anything at this time was access to a good library, where
he was thrilled to discover German translations of Homer, later
writing that 'he jumped for joy, kissed the book, pressed it to
his heart . . . took it into the school house, locked it up in a
drawer, and read in it, as often as he enjoyed a leisure moment
. . . he was determined to profit by it as much as possible.'[2]

However, possibly as a result of his peculiar teaching
method, his employment didn't last very long, and the years
which followed saw him moving between tailoring, tutoring
and threshing wheat, using his spare hours in the study of
maths, languages (including Greek and Hebrew) and agriculture. He was in his late twenties when his exasperated father,
no doubt frustrated by his son's apparent inability to settle into
a stable career, suggested that maybe he should consider studying medicine, and by good fortune, he was contacted by a close
friend of his father's, a Catholic priest who was coming to the
end of a successful career as an oculist, and who was looking for

someone to carry on his business. Jung-Stilling enthusiastically took on the challenge, and before very long had undertaken a successful eye operation on a 12-year-old boy; a period of medical studies at Strasbourg University led to a fine career as an eye doctor specializing in the removal of cataracts. Always on the move, he was appointed a few years later as lecturer on agriculture, technology, commerce and veterinary medicine at the University of Heidelberg, before moving to Marburg as professor of economic, financial and statistical studies; his father's hopes for a set career path were seemingly not something which Jung-Stilling shared.

By the second half of his life, Jung-Stilling's main focus was on spiritual matters. He had discovered the writings of Johann Albrecht Bengel, and also spent time with a group of Philadelphians who reportedly used Bengel's End Time 1836 calculation in their expectation of the Second Coming, which he adopted for his own prediction. Jung-Stilling reported that during Sunday afternoon meetings with the Philadelphians he felt that he was 'raptured to the third Heaven'.[3] Work and family life (he was married three times, widowed twice, with 13 children) were no deterrent to devoting his time to literary pursuits, and it is one of his novels which has particular significance to this history.

The book in question was a novel entitled *Heimweh* (Homesickness, or in this context, 'Longing for Heaven'), which came to him 'as if by chance' in the early 1790s.[4] He had been wondering how to present a series of maxims he had written which had been inspired by verses from the Bible, when a local bookseller encouraged him to write a book that could be guaranteed to sell successfully. Jung-Stilling used as his inspiration John Bunyan's *Pilgrim's Progress*, which had been published over a hundred years earlier, in 1678. Bunyan's tale tells of a pilgrim named Christian who is in search of 'that which is to come', implying the Celestial City atop Mount Zion, which is often understood as being a synonym for Jerusalem. Jung-Stilling decided to write a book 'which was intended to describe the wearisome journey of a Christian towards his eternal home', reporting that 'his state of mind, while he was engaged in this work, was peculiar indeed; his spirit seemed to be elevated into ethereal regions, and an indescribable sensation of a happy tranquility pervaded his soul. When he sat down to the work the ideas rushed so rapidly into his mind, that he was scarcely able to write fast enough, hence the work received a very different form and tendency from that at first contemplated.'[5]

Mirroring Bunyan's story, Jung-Stilling's hero, also named Christian, travels towards the east in his quest to find the ultimate land of peace where all good Christians would find a true home at the end of time, and he named this place Solyma.[6] Published between 1794 and 1796, the book was a raging success, Jung-Stilling proudly reporting in his autobiography:

> this work was uncommonly well received, many copies were sent to America, where it is frequently read. It became known in Asia, wherever there were Germans, friends to the Christian religion . . . many learned sceptics were thereby gained over to the Christian cause; in short, there are few books, which have excited so general an interest.[7]

Shortly after its publication Jung-Stilling received a visit from a young man to whom he refers simply as 'the remarkable N ---', and who had been seeking a meeting since reading the book in order to ask the author a burning question: 'how does it happen, that you are so well acquainted with the society which exists in the East, and describe it so accurately in your work, and point out so minutely their places of meeting in Egypt, on Mount Sinai in the monastery of Canobin, and under the Temple of Jerusalem?'[8]

Jung-Stilling's response was simply that he had absolutely no knowledge of such a society and that his novel was pure fiction, to which his visitor responded, 'pardon me, you have related nothing but the truth. It is incomprehensible to me, how you could so exactly hit it!' His account of the society in the East astonished Jung-Stilling, who tantalisingly reported that some 'remarkable and extraordinary circumstances' were 'not suitable for publication'. A letter from 'a certain sovereign' which also referred to the society in the East unfortunately met with the same response.[9]

Heimweh started out as a work of fiction, and certainly for the author this was his sole intention, simply a novel inspired by his conviction that God had in mind a safe haven for his faithful followers at the time of the end. However, almost as soon as the book was in print, he felt the need to produce an explanatory supplement in order to satisfy a readership which saw his book as prophetic in nature. Of particular interest to the reader was Jung-Stilling's allegorical reference to the final battle between good and evil, light and darkness, Christ and Satan, as mentioned in the Book of Revelation (19: 7–21 in particular), following which would come the time of the end and the return of Christ. Recent events, such as the French Revolution, which was regarded as causing the de-Christian-izing of France, and the rise of Napoleon, whom Jung-Stilling regarded as an apocalyptic figure, were the fuel for his belief in the proximity of the end times, and the foundation of his con-cept of Solyma as a refuge. In the novel, Solyma is situated near Samarkand, Central Asia (now Uzbekistan), as far away as he thought possible from Napoleon's influence, although by 1806 Jung-Stilling had moved Solyma further west, into Russia, which had already been a popular destination for Christians seeking religious freedom for several decades.

The following contemporary account, written in 1840, gives a flavour of what was taking place not long after *Heimweh* was published. Dr Pinkerton, to whom reference is made, and from whom the information was gleaned, was a respected mission-ary who in 1813 had helped found the Russian Bible Society in St Petersburg:

Among the German colonists in the vicinity of Odessa, some families of peasants from Wertemberg reached that country in the autumn of the year 1817, on their journey to Mount Ararat, whither they were induced to migrate from a religious *nostalgia*, though they were not themselves Jewish descendants. In January, 1818, Dr. Pinkerton met with two leaders of their sect in Moscow, named Koch and Frick, which city was then visited by the emperor and his family. They were deputed by the brethren to petition Alexander for assistance, whose piety and benevolence represented him to them as one raised up to prepare the kingdom of the Saviour upon earth . . . It appears that Professor Jung-Stilling, of Baden, was a popular prophetic writer of this persuasion, and probably the principal author of this enthusiastic and ill-timed attempt to forestall futurity . . . He fixed both the year and place of Christ's appearance and reign with such positiveness, that numbers sold their property, and hastened to the East in consequence. Bengel of Wertemberg was another author of the same too visionary character . . . Numbers of their infatuated followers removed to the south of Russia. At one time 7000 having placed their families' effects upon rafts in the Danube, with colours flying, and singing Millennial songs, arrived in the Black Sea; but before they had passed quarantine, and approached the place of their destination, nearly 3000 of them had perished by disease and hardship. The Emperor Alexander, with his wonted liberality, gave them money, allowed them a guide through the mountains of Caucasus into Georgia, and ordered that the Governor General should permit them to settle there, making them a grant from the crown lands. Koch and Frick both declared their implicit belief that they were really *inspired* to write ejaculatory effusions. The death of their companions did not quench the ardours of the pursuit, nor could they be dissuaded from their rash project, though they were apprized that the country where they had become settlers, was very unhealthy, and that the tribes there subsisted by robbery and murder.

Early in the spring of 1818, they passed Mount Caucasus, and planted themselves in some villages on the banks of the Kur, at some distance from Tiflis; but such were the difficulties which they encountered, and sickness they endured, that many of them were aroused from their imaginary speculation, and some of them altogether renounced their religious faith. The authorities of St Petersburg were made acquainted, by the Governor General, with the diseases to which they fell a prey. Frick died. Koch being reproached by the rest, fled to Sarepta on the Wolga, where he was glad to join the Moravians, who were sound in word and practice, and he grievously repented of the part which he had taken. The Basle Missionary Society sent pastors among the remainder of those poor people, who were otherwise left exposed on all sides. The most tragical part of their history, however, is still untold. In the war between Russia and Persia, they were subjected to a hostile invasion of their territory, and even treated with the most ignominious brutality. On the morning of the 26th of August, 1826, one thousand Turkish and Curdish horsemen attacked the colony of Catherinenfeld, forced their way through the gates, and commenced the ravages of the most uncivilized warfare . . . The scene is thus depicted by M. Saltête, a missionary:

'No human tongue can describe the misery which, in the course of a few hours, overwhelmed the settlement. Some of the colonists, in attempting to escape, were caught with long cords, in the same manner as wild cattle. Whoever was taken was thus immediately stripped of his clothing, and either killed on the spot, or suffered to run away naked. Little children were bound together in couples, and then slung across the horses' backs, like articles of baggage. If any of them disturbed their persecutors by their cries, they were instantly dispatched, before the face of their parents. Every sense of shame, and every feeling of humanity, was extinguished in these barbarians; the brutal herds set no limits to their licentious passions. A young woman, of acknowledged piety, in endeavouring to escape from the robbers, was fired at and shot in the spine; so that she instantly fell, and slowly expired, in the most excruciating agonies, on the ground. A man, whilst endeavouring to intercede for the lives of his wife and children, was murdered at the foot of a tree, to which his wife had fled for shelter. The latter, with an infant at the breast, was spared; but with a bleeding heart she saw her two little ones carried away into slavery. Three girls, about fifteen years of age, thought themselves happy in having reached the river, at a distance of about seven or eight versts; when two Tartars overtook them, and cruelly wreaked their vengeance on two of them. Among the wounded, who were afterwards taken up and attended to, was one who had his skull laid open, and was wounded in the back with no less than twenty-two thrusts of a lance. A Curd ordered another of the colonists to throw himself on the ground, in which situation he pierced him twice with a lance, in the same manner as fishes are caught by spearing in the water: another Curd hurled a large stone at him, so that he was eventually left half dead. The most deplorable situation was that of the poor captives, who were treated like brutes, and inhumanly butchered, if they did not immediately obey the cruel orders of the plunderers. A part of them have been carried away, and sold in Turkey, and the remainder are in slavery in Persia. The Almighty hand of the Lord, however, preserved the lives of 240 persons; but upwards of thirty were put to death, and about 140 were carried away into slavery.'[10]

Two years later, in 1842, the above article appeared in the *British North American Wesleyan Methodist Magazine*, preceded by the following paragraph:

Popular delusions have been innumerable – every age of the world having contributed its share of folly to the general mass. And much is it to be lamented, that the Church of God, although assuming higher principles – to be governed by holier motives, and guided by inspired instruction, has not been wanting in her efforts to impose upon weak and unstudious minds: – witness the monstrous catalogue of heresies which pollute the pages of Ecclesiastical History ... The final apostasy – the battle of Armageddon – The return of the Jews to Palestine – The personal rein of Christ for a thousand years on this earth, are no more the Gospel of Christ, than the worshipping of the Aaronic calf, the destruction of the Canaanitish nations, and the imperial reign of Solomon, were the Law of Moses ...

... For of what consequence can it be to anyone dying now, (and who is freed from the exposure to instant death?) whether in 1842, or a thousand years subsequently, the dreaming rein of enthusiasts be accomplished?[11]

It was Tzar Alexander's grandmother, Catherine the Great, who had first encouraged settlement in Russia, hoping to open up uncultivated regions of the country and increase the population. Invitations were sent out all over Europe in the early 1760s, offering free land and religious liberty, with the result that within a few years approximately 27,000 German settlers had arrived, with 106 colonies established along the Volga river close to Saratov providing separate villages for Protestant and Catholic denominations. Alexander I continued his grandmother's initiative, his 1804 manifesto inviting thousands to leave their homes for a better and freer life in Russia, with many arriving from Württemberg, where Pietist groups were dissatisfied with the established church.

Alexander met Jung-Stilling towards the end of a long period of political turmoil which culminated in Napoleon's defeat and abdication in April 1814, following Alexander's triumphal entry into Paris a month earlier. Appalled by the atrocities and devastation of war, Alexander now turned to his religious faith, and it was at this time that he formed what he considered to be a deep and significant relationship with Jung-Stilling, whose employer at the time just happened to be the brother of Alexander's wife. Alexander had hoped to meet Jung-Stilling during a visit to Karlsruhe in 1813, but time being short, the visit was postponed until July 1814. On 9 July, with several other guests, Jung-Stilling was invited to dine with Alexander at Bruchsal Castle in Württemberg, followed by a long private meeting on the 10th, a meeting which according to contemporary records was memorable to the point of being astonishing. Both political and religious matters were discussed, topics including God's Kingdom, the immediate future and the practice of true religion. Alexander's relationship with Jung-Stilling was remarkable enough, but even more remarkable was an association which followed shortly afterwards, related to both Jung-Stilling and Alexander and involving an extraordinary woman by the name of Baroness Barbara Juliana von Krüdener, who through birth and marriage was extremely well-connected and well-travelled, as well as enjoying a degree of success as an authoress. Her strange, eccentric and bizarre life left its mark on a period of history already teaming with political and religious intrigue.

3

'The Reign of Christ Will Come, Sire': Baroness Barbara Juliana Von Krüdener

Watch therefore: for ye know not what hour your Lord doth come.

Matt. 24:42

Barbara Juliana's marriage at the age of 18 to Baron von Krüdener, 16 years her senior, was based more on convenience than love, and although she found herself plunged into a succession of cosmopolitan encounters through her husband's eminent position in the Russian Diplomatic Service, this was in no way a substitute for the romance and excitement she both lacked and craved. She was entering her 40s when, in 1804–5, her life took an altogether more dramatic direction as a result of a spiritual conversation with her shoemaker, who happened to be a devout member of the Moravian Brethren, and who inspired her to take the mystic and evangelical path. In 1807 she paid a visit to the Moravian settlement at Herrnhut, after which she and her two daughters resided for a while in the home of Jung-Stilling in Karlsruhe, imbibing Pietist thought in the process and undoubtedly exposed to Bengel's doctrine regarding the end times and the imminence of Christ's return; such was the intensity of her experience in the Jung-Stilling home that she was tempted to stay for ever. Time in Karlsruhe was also spent at the residence of the Court of Baden, where she was able to share her newly found beliefs among those who, due to the threatening behaviour of Napoleon as he swept through Europe, were open to the voice of religion; most notable amongst her listeners were several queens, including those from Sweden, Bavaria, Hanover and Holland, this last being none other than the stepdaughter of Napoleon himself.

Baroness Barbara Juliana Von Krüdener

The life of the Baroness took yet another dramatic turn in 1809 when she met up with a charismatic Pietist minister of dubious repute, one Jean-Frédéric Fontaines, who had in tow a clairvoyant named Marie Kummrin, a peasant woman of little education who lost no time in foretelling that the Baroness's immediate destiny was to buy an estate where a colony of the 'elect' would gather in order to wait for 'the coming of the Lord', and from where they would spread their teachings throughout Germany. Unfortunately, the Baroness plunged herself into the scheme, buying an estate which Maria Kummrin declared was the decree of God, as she and Fontaines promptly installed themselves. Despite her seemingly reckless behaviour, opinions of the Baroness nevertheless overflowed with enthusiasm:

> Her rank, her reckless charities, and her exuberant eloquence produced a great effect on the simple country folk . . . many wretched peasants sold or distributed all they possessed and followed the Baroness and Fontaines into Württemberg, where the settlement was established at Catharinenplaisir and the château of Bönnigheim . . . [1]

No doubt spurred on by her apparent successes, clairvoyant Marie excelled herself when she announced publicly that Napoleon would elevate the status of the Duke of Württemberg to that of king; however, despite her prediction coming true, the new king was keen to show that his elevated position had nothing to do with Maria Kummrin at all, and promptly sent her to prison. When the Baroness spoke to Marie through her prison window, the king banished her from Württemberg and dispersed the colony at Bönnigheim, although seemingly the Baroness's influence was sufficient in helping them to establish a new home in the neighbouring state of Baden. Unfortunately this episode in no way alerted the Baroness to Fontaines' true character, or indeed, to that of his accomplice Marie Kummrin, for shortly afterwards, having moved to a church in Karlsruhe where he had been appointed minister, the cunning duo managed to persuade the Baroness to open a new institution which they quickly occupied, the only outcome being a considerable loss of money for their trusting Baroness.

But the tide was turning, and 'the influence of Fontaines, to whom she had been "spiritually married" (Madame Fontaines being content with the part of Martha in the household, so long as the baroness's funds lasted), had now waned'.[2] However, as far as the Baroness's own destiny was concerned, 'her preaching and her indiscriminate charities now began to attract curious crowds from afar; and her appearance everywhere was accompanied by an epidemic of visions and prophesyings, which culminated in the appearance in 1811 of the comet, a sure sign of the approaching end'.[3]

Two years later Baroness von Krüdener was residing in Geneva, where she spent some time deepening the faith of a group of young Pietists, one of whom was Henri Louis Empeytaz, a theological student who was later destined to play a significant part in what she considered to be a triumphant period in her extraordinary spiritual quest, involving none other than Tzar Alexander of Russia himself. Empeytaz was involved in founding a new sect in Geneva, a group of Calvinistic Methodists known as the Momiers who were keen to break away from the teachings of the official church, and in conjunction with his attendances at the Baroness's prayer meetings this served to end his relationship with the university. However, the Baroness was obviously impressed by him, for not long afterwards he 'officiated in the family of Madame de Krudener', something which appears to have been a more or less full-time occupation.[4]

The Baroness was on fire with spiritual conviction, and she was determined to take her ideas and beliefs to the people who were in a position to change the course of history. The French Revolution and Napoleonic Wars had caused havoc and misery all over Europe; but the success of the Battle of the Nations in October 1813, led by Alexander I, which defeated the French army of Napoleon and led to Napoleon's abdication and exile to the island of Elba, had seemed to be a turning point in European politics, and in November 1814 European ambassadors gathered at the Congress of Vienna in order to negotiate a plan for long-term peace. Looking for an opportunity to make her mark,

> Madame von Krüdener's eye began to turn on the Emperor Alexander as the one of the Royal personages on whom there was a hope of operating towards a better state of things. He had the reputation of piety; and with her ardent and believing nature, she persuaded herself that by an earnest appeal, supported by the blessing of God, he might be induced to commence the work of a genuine reformation of society. The more she dwelt on this idea, the more her mind kindled upon it.[5]

The Baroness had already met Tzar Alexander through her husband's position in the Russian court, and she also knew Roxane de Stourdza, who was maid of honour to Alexander's wife, and to whom she now wrote an urgent letter in the hope that an interview with the Emperor could be arranged. Since Roxane's brother was Alexander's private secretary, the request and subsequent emotionally charged letters voicing her concern for the future, which included her belief that Napoleon was about to escape from Elba and that the 'bloodshed of the year 1815 would be more dreadful than ever',[6] were duly delivered to the Tzar. True to her predictions, Napoleon escaped from Elba in February 1815, making a grand entrance in Paris on 20 March. Seven days earlier, representatives of the great Powers of Europe had gathered in order to declare him an enemy of world peace, agreeing to eliminate him once and for all and manoeuvring their armies towards France in preparation for war.

In the spring of 1815 the Baroness was residing at Schlüchtern, Baden-Württemberg, where she was in the process of encouraging local peasants to sell everything they had in order to escape the brewing storm. When she heard that Alexander was staying in nearby Heilbronn on his way to France, she was determined to meet him, and on 4 June her wish was granted. There are several recorded reports of what took place and the aftermath, one of which states:

> To the tsar, who had been brooding alone over an open Bible, her sudden arrival seemed an answer to his prayers; for three hours the prophetess preached her strange gospel, while the most powerful man in Europe sat, his face buried in his hands, sobbing like a child; until at last he declared that he had found peace.[7]

When Alexander moved to Heidelberg on his way to Paris he took a small house near the city, inviting the Baroness to follow him, which she did, renting a villa nearby.

> To that humble abode Alexander came every other evening after the business of the day, at ten o'clock, and remained till two o'clock in the morning, joining with Madame de Krudener's

family, in which M. Empeytaz officiated as chaplain, in reading the Scriptures, prayer, and religious conversation; politics and all other secular subjects being utterly excluded . . . So anxious was the Emperor to advance in the knowledge of Divine truth that he was always the first to point our suitable parts of Scripture for discussion . . .[8]

It was whilst Alexander was enjoying this spiritual haven in Heidelberg that news came of the decisive Battle at Waterloo and final defeat of Napoleon on 18 June, after which the triumphant kings of Europe moved quickly to Paris.

Being about to depart for France, the Emperor requested that Madame de Krudener's family would follow him, and gave them passports for that purpose. After remaining a short time in the grand duchy of Baden till the roads were clear, they proceeded by circuitous routes to avoid places still occupied by Napoleon's troops; and after a very difficult journey through provinces laid waste, and villages destroyed, they arrived at Paris on the 14th of July. The following day Madame de Krudener hastened to pay her dutiful homage to her sovereign, and had the consolation of finding him strengthened in the way of salvation. He requested that her family would settle near his residence, since he wished to continue the religious intercourse commenced at Heidelberg. Accordingly, the Emperor having chosen the Elisée-Bourbon palace for his residence, Madame de Krudener's family settled in the hôtel Montchenu, the garden of which communicated with that of the Elisée Bourbon; and the Emperor, passing through those gardens, continued the religious interviews every other evening.[9]

Empeytaz was still with the Baroness (sometimes referred to as Madame de Krüdener) at this juncture, and every evening the emperor went to take part in the prayer meetings conducted by the Baroness and Empeytaz. 'Chiliasm seemed to have found an entrance into the high councils of Europe, and the baroness von Krüdener had become a political force to be reckoned with. Admission to her religious gatherings was sought by a crowd of people celebrated in the intellectual and social world'; these meetings also 'attracted other members of the chiliastic fraternity, among them Fontaines, who brought with him the prophetess Marie Kummrin'.[10]

> Here then we reach that point of our heroine's life, which fixed upon her the eyes and wonder of all Europe. Three times a week she held religious meetings in the Hotel Montchenu which were attended by all the princes, ministers and great generals of Europe . . . There she addressed the assembled Powers of Europe in an animated eloquence calling upon them in the plainest terms of the Gospel to put an end to the horrors which had so long made wretched the world, by adopting fully and effectively the principles of Christianity. To accept Christ in his completeness, and thus inaugurate the reign of peace and freedom on the earth . . . In private she laboured with Alexander to induce him to establish a real reign of Christ in his dominions, and to use his efforts with his brother monarchs to do the same in theirs.[11]

'The reign of Christ', she said, 'will come, sire. Glory and honour to those who fight for Him! Form a holy alliance of all those who belong to the true faith, and let them take an oath to combat the innovators who wish to overthrow religion, and you will triumph eternally with it.'[12]

It was in this intense atmosphere that a seed was sown which blossomed to become the Holy Alliance, proclaimed on 26 September 1815 and signed by the sovereigns of Russia, Austria and Prussia. It was Alexander himself who instigated the Alliance in order to promote peace by introducing Christian principles into national affairs, although the Baroness declared herself to be the brain behind it; whether or not this was true, her relationship with Alexander and the influence she and

Empeytaz undoubtably had on his thinking certainly played a part. The Alliance was later endorsed by all the monarchs of Europe, apart from the Pope, who eschewed any treaty involving Protestant Kings, the Sultan of Turkey, or the King of Great Britain, on constitutional grounds.

For a number of reasons the Holy Alliance eventually fizzled out and became defunct with Alexander's death in 1825, although his faith in Baroness von Krüdener had already been dealt a blow during one of their meetings in Paris as the Alliance was still in its embryonic state. Attending the meeting was the clairvoyant Marie Kummrin, who announced in a trance that God's wish for Alexander was that he should finance the religious community in which she lived, his response being that 'he had received too many such revelations before to be impressed'.[13] The relationship between Alexander and his Baroness was all but finished, and although before he left Paris he gave her a passport to Russia, she never saw him again.

The final years weren't at all easy for Baroness von Krüdener, as she found herself being expelled first from Switzerland, and then from one German state after another as her health gradually declined. In 1818 she returned to her estate in Kosse, Livonia (now Viitina, Estonia), followed by a brief visit to St Petersburg where she attempted to persuade Alexander of his divine mission to take up arms on behalf of Christendom.[14] His response to this passionate request, however, was a long polite letter in which he told her that she should leave St Petersburg at once. Back on her estate the Baroness's already fragile health steadily declined, although this was in no way a deterrent to one final religious act, for when in the spring of 1824 she was invited to participate in the founding of a Christian colony in the Crimea, she didn't hesitate. The long and arduous journey, part of which involved travelling by boat, was too much for the Baroness, and with the care of her daughter she spent the final months of her life in the small town of Karasu-Bazar, where she passed away on Christmas Eve, 1824.

Baroness von Krüdener's belief in Chiliasm ran like a thread through all her Christian activities, as it did for so many Christians living in Europe at the time; indeed, the turbulent political situation in Europe inspired and galvanized a steady stream of Christians who believed that the end times were close and who, for a variety of reasons, chose to move towards the east in order to create perfect Christian communities. This sentiment was common in several areas of Christian society, and it is to one in particular that our focus now moves. Later known by the name, German Templers, it not only had its own specific remarkable agenda, but also a driving passion to fulfil that agenda whatever the obstacles which presented themselves.

The story of the German Templers began in south-west Germany, and their journey eventually led them towards the Holy Land, where a small group of Bahá'ís and their leader, Bahá'u'lláh, had recently arrived at the prison city of Akka. Although unimaginable challenges awaited both the Bahá'ís and the Templers, it is to the Templers that we now turn, beginning with the early life of the man who was instrumental in making his dream into reality; his name was Christoph Hoffmann.

4

'Thy Kingdom Come':[1]
Christoph Hoffmann

And as he sat upon the mount of Olives, the disciples came unto
him privately, saying,
Tell us, when shall these things be? and what shall be the sign of
thy coming,
and of the end of the world?
Matt. 24:3

Christoph Hoffmann, founder of the German Templers, was
born in Leonberg, in the Kingdom of Württemberg, south-west-
ern Germany, in 1815. Six years earlier the new king, Frederick
I, had caused great upset in the Christian community when he
introduced a new pattern of church worship, which excluded
the church from any decision making and changed fundamental religious practices. These measures were viewed as being the
final straw by Christians who had already endured the appearance in 1791 of the 'Enlightenment Hymnbook' with its dull
replacements of spiritually uplifting hymns, and following the
severe hardships endured during the Napoleonic Wars. This
latest development gave many Pietists reason enough to escape
in order to seek a new and better life elsewhere. Although the
situation eased in 1816 when King Frederick was succeeded by
his son, William I, hundreds of Christians continued to flee to
any country which would accept them, including Russia and
America, Christoph Hoffmann later writing,

> With all their family and means good citizens left, hoping to
> find countries where no one could interfere with their beliefs
> . . . The famine in that same year [1817] caused additional
> numbers to leave. The way to Jerusalem, then under Turkish

rule, was closed, and those who believed that the Kingdom of God should center there made the long trek to Russia as a temporary detour, to await a hoped-for later possibility.[2]

Christoph Hoffmann spent the first few years of his life in Leonberg, where his father, Gottlieb Wilhelm Hoffmann (1771–1846) was Burgermeister and consultant to the Court of Württemberg. Gottlieb had been greatly influenced by Pietist thinking, and spent his free time reading all the religious books he could lay his hands on, including those of Bengel, Oetinger, Hahn, Zinzendorf, and Jakob Böhme (see Chapter 1). Gottlieb also led a group of intellectuals with almost daily meetings in his home, Hoffmann later noting that

> around 1795, as a result of advising and assisting many families during the difficult period of the rise of Napoleon, he was elected to the office of Mayor. Always people kept asking of him, 'what can we do?'. Sometimes the gatherings grew so large that the house was too small and they would go into the woods or meet in the court chambers at night. They called each other *Brethren* – the name suited them. About this time a Pastor Friedrich joined the Leonberg Community of Brethren. He was an enthusiastic preacher and his sermons upheld mostly the Bengel conception of the future of the Children of God. He stressed especially the prophecy of the rebuilding of Jerusalem, with Palestine to become the central point of all worship.[3]

Alarmed by the steady stream of inhabitants joining the flow of emigrants from his realm, the new young King William of Württemberg called together his most trusted officials, including Gottlieb, who was quick to point out what he regarded as the causes for this exodus, the main reason being that many Christians were extremely upset by the introduction of new religious practices, causing them to feel 'estranged from the church and thereby conscientiously oppressed'. Gottlieb suggested that if the King allowed them to worship as they wished then perhaps they could be persuaded to stay, offering 'to draw up a plan for a designated area, to be administered under a special dispensation, permitting the use of the old form of confessional'. The government responded immediately by asking for numbers, Gottlieb providing them with a 'long lists of signatures, not only of Leonberg Brethren, but from numerous villages and hamlets nearby'.[4]

As a result of these interventions the King authorized a special community for the Brethren in 1818, with Gottlieb as general manager and Pastor Friedrich as spiritual leader. The place chosen for this new venture was Korntal, a beautiful estate just north of Stuttgart, complete with castle, gardens, dairy and stables. Gottlieb's intention was to create a community inspired by the first Christians, based on the teachings of Christ; the architecture was simple, including that of the community hall, in which the eastern wall was inscribed with the words '"Yes, I am coming soon." Amen. Come, Lord Jesus' (Rev. 22:20), no doubt in keeping with the current hope of Christ's imminent return. Christoph Hoffmann later recorded:

> Korntal's customs and ceremonies had the homely charm of true devotion. Surely they must have affected other youth the way they did me, binding us with strong ties to this quiet place . . . The district school was the first building to be completed. There were dormitories for teachers and boarding students. After this, a girls' school was built. Then came a boarding school for neglected children, which was very close to father's heart. Also, a rest home for mental patients proved exceptionally successful. Father had the conviction that love and kindness were most important in their treatment. Korntal seemed to have a healing atmosphere – all peace and harmony. It was like an Ark, besieged on all sides by lost and fearful people seeking help.[5]

And it's here that we catch a glimpse of the young Hoffmann as a schoolboy at Korntal, when he notes that:

> My little carved animals were still dear to me in spite of reading Homer . . . Before School time I'd pick one of my little carved treasures, usually the orangutang, keeping him in my pocket. At my desk I built a cave for him of books with a secret crevice through which I could catch glimpses of him without missing one iota of the lesson in progress.[6]

One of the key beliefs of the Korntal community was that Christ would return in the year 1836, based on the predictions of Johann Albrecht Bengel; indeed, this expected event was just a couple of decades away as Korntal was being created. Hoffmann remembered that

> when I was six years old I was permitted to accompany my father to the *'Men's News Hour'*. Keeping pace with current events was important to the Brethren since all their opinions centered around Bengel's calculations. I recall *the first shots fired* at Moldavia [Greek War of Independence] in 1821 by Alexander Ypsilanti,[7] with Russian support. Now this appeared to be a *sign of the times* forshadowing the coming of the Kingdom of God. According to Bengel the signs should first appear in the orient.[8]

A little later, when a few in the community expressed their opinion that 'the true sanctuary for the Children of God was in Russia after all', Gottlieb exclaimed, '"don't you realise that the Scriptures say the gathering place for the *Children of God is in Jerusalem?*" But they considered the argument academic. Bengel's date for the "Day of Decision" was drawing closer – 1836.'[9]

When King William paid a visit to Korntal he was so impressed that he gave permission for similar communities to be established in other areas. Although certain factions in the government were very much opposed to such a proposition, they were prepared to consider it if it were to be a reclamation project involving a specific patch of moorland situated about a hundred miles south of Korntal. Gottlieb accepted the challenge, and once the land had been drained a self-supporting colony was established, named Wilhelmsdorf in honour of the king, with the chapel being dedicated in July 1828. Young Christoph Hoffmann often accompanied his father on visits to Wilhelmsdorf, on one occasion resting overnight 'at Kleinengstingen, where a settlement of Pietists were waiting to hear Father speak about the biblical prophesies and *signs of the times*'.[10]

It was in 1828 that Beate Paulus, following the death of her husband, Karl Friedrich, moved with her large family to Korntal, a move which proved to be significant to the young Hoffmann in the ensuing years. Beate was the daughter of watchmaker, inventor and theologian Philip Matthaus Hahn, the contemporary of Bengel who had constructed an astronomical clock using Bengel's eschatological calculations. This close relationship with Hahn's daughter and family was probably enhanced by the fact that Hoffmann was already attracted to Hahn's theological writings. Of his relationship with the Paulus family Hoffmann later wrote, 'our minds and intellects matched each other without any touchiness: never a desire to hurt each other with a pointed remark, nor did anyone ever think of taking anything personally. So refreshing! Not stiff and formal as it was in the Hoffmann establishment.'[11] This relationship with the Paulus sons, especially Immanuel, with whom he shared a close friendship early on, was to become increasingly important to Hoffmann as he moved through his teenage years and into adulthood.

When the time came for Hoffmann to decide on a career, he chose theology, and having spent his early teenage years at grammar school in Stuttgart, he entered Tübingen University in 1832, at the age of 17. This was a decisive and defining time in several ways for Hoffmann as he moved away from the influence of family and Korntal, finding himself exposed to religious and philosophical ideas outside his limited experience. His elder brother Wilhelm was serving as a tutor at the time, as was a former classmate of his, David Friedrich Strauss, who a few years later became somewhat of a sensation with his book *The Life of Jesus*, in which he denied the divinity of Christ, arguing that the New Testament miracles had no factual basis and had been added later. Indeed, there was already consternation amongst many Christians as to whether the view of Hegel, the great philosopher,[12] regarding the subject of immortality, was consistent with Christian eschatological doctrine in relation to the resurrection of the dead at the end of time, after the Second Coming, and Pietist evangelical communities in Württemberg were extremely shocked by what they saw as modern standpoints concerning established Christian belief. The revolutionary Christian views of Strauss, and his university course on Hegelian philosophy, did, however, fulfil a need, for there were students at the university who sought new directions and 'were striving against the old fundamental and steadfast views of the past'.[13]

In his own studies, which included 'the influence of their own religion on the lives of the Greeks', Hoffmann was 'amazed at the variety and how impressive were the ideas contained in oriental religions', commenting on his 'persistent, distant vision of the tremendous importance of religion in the development of mankind'.[14] However, Hoffmann still struggled with his personal faith, noting that his

> Pietist conscience caused me no little inner confusion: the impression remained strong that worldly arts were sinful. Now and then I realized the narrow outlook of this viewpoint. This conflict of two opposite spiritual concepts, wavering not only within me, but everywhere, seemed to manifest itself even in

my reading and in the life about me . . . I wrote one piece of poetry after another during this period, but found no satisfaction either intellectually or emotionally in these attempts to reconcile my fantastic imaginings imprisoned within my mental horizon. The inner Kaleidoscoping tumult was almost unbearable.[15]

In discussions with fellow students a friend advised Hoffmann that 'there's a danger in constantly questioning the rightness of religion, or whether the Christian religion might be perfected. Take it on faith!' After some thought, Hoffmann 'returned to an image of the Beyond, giving up Hegel's denial of immortality. We took our courses in *Philosophy of religion and Apologetics* very seriously now, striving to gain a true judgement of the Christian verities.' He also read 'examples of Oriental mystic poetry, fragments of sheer beauty, translated from *Djelaledin Rumi*, that remained unforgettable' in his mind.[16]

Amongst the students at Tübingen University seeking new ways of thinking were a group whose radical ideas appeared to threaten the authorities, who reciprocated by sending a military contingent into the university grounds early one morning. Hoffmann watched from the safety of his room as hundreds of students attempted to stop the soldiers in their tracks, but their efforts were to no avail, and many students were arrested and taken to prison. One of them was Georg David Hardegg, who served over six years as a political prisoner, and who was later to become Hoffmann's friend and associate in the Temple Society.

Meanwhile, Hoffmann diligently attended to his studies, which involved practising his preaching skills in the university auditorium before being let loose 'at hospitals, at sick beds, death beds and funerals, and all the other ceremonies of the church'.[17] This was followed during the holidays by some teaching at the Sunday school at Korntal, where a devastating typhoid outbreak had just recently forced the Latin

school (in effect, the boys' school) to close, causing consternation amongst the whole community. It was when three of
the Paulus brothers, including his close friend Immanuel, were
invited to re-establish the school that Hoffmann wondered if
there might be a place for him in this exciting undertaking,
later remembering, 'my dreams were filled with hope for such
a realization: to be *part* of a school of the highest ideals and
standards.'[18] He continued,

> we had more faith in our future, Immanuel and I confided
> to each other as we walked back to the university after these
> holidays in Korntal. Gradually we understood that a mere
> acceptance and a repetition of mystical formulas about
> Christianity lacked the true substance. Our thinking, we
> agreed, needed to be brought to the point of a new positive
> philosophy tenable against the more popular Hegelian view.
> Reading the Strauss *Life of Jesus* carefully, I wondered that
> the book had aroused so much attention. Cleverly compiled
> quotations, mostly garnered from the works of other critics
> of the New Testament, made up the greater part of the work.
> The rest consisted of a list of the so-called inconsistencies in
> the Gospels. It brings no understanding for the postulates of
> practical reasoning, the main requirement in religion. I was
> amazed that listing superficialities to serve as ammunition
> against the Christian religion should seem seriously conclusive
> to the author. Evidently Professor Strauss had not conceived to
> prove an ideal of Christ but an ideal of Hegel. Naturally, the
> Pietist students in the group were just as shocked as I at the
> closing chapter of the book, in which the professor suggests
> doing away with the Bible entirely. It seemed strange that the
> volume should be so popular. *I determined to seek a new foun-
> dation for philosophical research that would be more solid than
> Hegel's.*[19]

When Hoffmann's brother Wilhelm wrote an article in response to Strauss's book on Christ, he took the viewpoint of modern orthodox theology, 'in a manner as though orthodox theology held all the keys to all questions, riddles, and mysteries of life'. Hoffmann's opinion was that 'it was not a convincing viewpoint, even though perhaps my demands were too high. Where are the answers to those questions that arise from the very depth of one's soul? . . . somewhere there must be a region, a *Kingdom of God* attainable for all mankind.'[20]

As the year 1836 approached anticipation rose amongst the Pietists of Württemberg. Hoffmann later remembered,

> while we students and younger Pietists at Tübingen were not deeply touched by Bengel's prediction, we knew that in Korntal the revelatory themes were a subject of great concern. But, there was no sign of a great migration to Jerusalem as prophecies predicted, while the greater part of the world was to be submerged in trials and tribulations. And no sign of any approaching judgment.[21]

Although Bengel's predictions appear to be, to all intents and purposes, the only ones which the Pietists in Hoffman's circle adhered to, Bengel was far from being the only theologian in Germany who had written on the subject. An article written towards the end of the 19th century sheds some light on other voices commenting on the Second Coming of Christ during the first half of the century:

> The most of our readers have perhaps heard of the noted Lutheran prelate Bengel, who in the last century fixed the time of our Lord's appearing in the year 1836, his calculations being based on the number 666 in the revelation. But long ere this time expired, another man began to write, the chief schoolmaster, named Leonard Heinrich Kelber. His first pamphlet appeared in 1824, called 'The End Near', containing an exposition of Matthew 24 and 25. It was printed in Bavaria. But

in 1835 a larger pamphlet, with the same title, appeared in Stuttgart, containing 126 pages.

Given that Korntal was situated just to the north of Stuttgart, it's hard to believe that the community there wasn't aware of Kelber's comments on Bengel's predictions; if they were, it appears that they chose to ignore them, which is curious given the strong message in Kelber's 1835 version of the pamphlet, which states on the title page,

> The End Comes, proven in a thorough and convincing manner from the word of God and the latest events; invalidating totally all prejudice against waiting for the coming of our Lord, or reckoning of the time, showing plainly how prelate Bengel erred seven years in reference to the great decisive year; for not 1836, but the year 1843, is the terminus, at which the great struggle between light and darkness will be finished, and the long expected reign of peace of our Lord Jesus will commence on earth.

In 1842 Kelber produced an even larger pamphlet in Stuttgart, this time with 286 pages, the long title ending with the words, 'the nearness of our Lord to judge antichrist – the great and joyful event of the year 1843'.[22]

In the meantime, Hoffmann's attention was focused on the new boys' school being planned at Korntal by the Paulus sons, particularly in regard to his possible involvement, and although his father knew and respected the Paulus family, his opinion was that their university education merited higher achievements than the boys' school at Korntal. Indeed, when young Christoph Paulus gave up a promising career with the State of Württemberg in order to teach at the Paulus School, Gottlieb Hoffmann was so appalled that he 'walked over to the Paulus home with great determined strides' to speak to Christoph's mother, feeling that as the leader of Korntal it was 'his duty to point out these ominous mistakes'.

It was while Christoph Hoffmann was away teaching at a private academy for a year that the Paulus school drama came to a head. Permission for extra space at Korntal had been denied by the Korntal Council, but a committee from nearby Ludwigsberg stepped in and offered a beautiful site which later became known as the Salon. Hoffmann's mother had tried to persuade him to stay at Korntal, and although his father disapproved of this new venture he did, nevertheless, allow him to choose his own path, commenting in a letter, 'it seems a dangerous step for your inner life, also for your outward life. I shall never cease to pray for you . . .'[23]

The Salon school was very much a Paulus family initiative; all the brothers were involved in teaching, and significant responsibilities were given to their sisters, as well as to their mother, Beate, 'upon whose faith the entire undertaking had rested from the beginning'. Hoffmann was involved in teaching at the school from its inception in 1837, and it was during this period that he formed a romantic attachment to Beate's youngest daughter, Pauline Paulus, of whom he wrote, 'her gentle disposition, her innate taste for beauty and order, her organizational talent and good judgment, had endeared her to me'.[24] In 1840 Hoffmann was called back to Tübingen in order to fulfil his obligation to serve as a tutor for a couple of terms, and a year later, at aged 22, he was married to Pauline, later remembering, 'unforgettable . . . was the feel of Pauline's small hand in mine, giving me a new sense of responsibility'.[25]

Shortly after his wedding Hoffmann took up his place as a teacher of philosophy and history at the Salon school, noting that

> novels and comedies usually end with the wedding. In reality, however, his marriage marks the beginning of a man's career – *his destiny*. My story is my journey to Jerusalem; and, being readied by God who shaped the circumstances that led me from Wuerttemberg to Jerusalem.[26]

Christoph Hoffmann with his wife Pauline and their son Seth

When, in 1842, Beate Paulus died of pneumonia, Hoffmann wrote an essay in her memory, the response in the newspapers from a Professor Vischer being the catalyst for what very quickly became an ardent dispute. Friedrich Theodor Vischer was a friend of David Friedrich Strauss, and when Vischer became professor of aesthetics at Tübingen in 1844 his inaugural address, in which he openly confessed to pantheism, not only caused uproar from Church and press alike, but also led to two years' suspension by the Württemberg government.[27]

Hoffmann was one of many who made their voices heard, contributing an open letter to a newspaper entitled: 'Twenty-one Sentences to refute the Deniers of God'[28] and condemning anyone confessing a belief in pantheism as blasphemers and idolaters. The epic dispute which erupted between Vischer and his friends on the one hand and Hoffmann and the Paulus brothers on the other was the catalyst which opened the door to the founding of a new magazine, fulfilling the 'need for a religious organ, free and courageous, able to stand against the growing unbelief of professor Vischer and the horde of enemies of Christianity'.[29] The *Süddeutsche Warte* (*South-German Sentinel*) was duly launched in May 1845, Hoffmann's numerous articles soon gaining him recognition further away from home. His scathing criticism of both the official Church and conditions generally were countered by his promotion of a Christian State and social order, his sentiments attracting strong support, particularly amongst Pietists living in the countryside at a time when general unrest was causing consternation amongst the whole population.

At home, Hoffmann spent precious time with his dying father, himself falling ill with rheumatic fever shortly after Gottlieb's death. It was during this quiet moment that he read again Jung-Stilling's autobiography, a book which impressed him so much that he returned to it again and again. And when, early in 1848, liberal protesters rose up against the establishment all over Europe, Hoffmann noted that 'several skirmishes took place on the streets of Ludwigsberg and the grounds of the Salon',[30] and expressed the hope that this revolutionary outbreak would make possible the construction of both State and society on a strong Christian foundation. One of the chief revolutionaries just happened to be David Friedrich Strauss, and when he put his name forward for a seat in the new parliament in Frankfurt, Hoffmann was invited to run against him and won with a large majority. However, he soon realized that his expectations for a Christian State were no more than a dream, and following a testing ten months in Frankfurt he returned to the Salon.

The political upheavals of 1848 had inspired Hoffmann to take a deeper look at Biblical prophecy, and in doing so he now viewed the revolutionary movement as being a modern

Tower of Babel, humanity's move away from God and religion, driving it forwards into the inevitable abyss. In 1849 he produced a pamphlet with the title *Voices of Prophecy regarding Babylon and God's People*, expressing his growing belief that humanity could only avoid a repetition of Babylon if there was a gathering of God's people in a Christian community.[31] The gathering together of God's people was now, more than ever, on Hoffmann's mind, as was his belief in the imminent Second Coming of Christ, which according to his reading of Biblical prophecy would take place in Jerusalem; and it was in Jerusalem, he believed, that God's people were to gather, far away from the influence of the corrupt west, and a symbol of the rebuilding of the temple. However, 1836 had long passed, and although Bengel's prediction of the Second Coming had apparently been unfruitful, this didn't appear to effect Hoffmann's resolve.

During this period his soul-searching led him to a life-changing decision:

more and more this question became my concern: *how could our Christian religion be revitalized? How cure it of its feckless existence?* Philipp and Immanuel were in accord with me at first that the Sentinel should follow this theme from now on with intensive zeal. It was before I had ever thought of stepping out of the State Church, and long before I had given the idea of colonization in foreign countries any consideration, that my lead article in the Sentinel was headed: 'Christianity in the First Century'. While it had been my intention merely to alert the readers to a more spiritual life, the article stirred up a storm. The article was said to hold political implications; there were reactions from every direction. We were accused of seditious leanings. I was at once in the midst of a fight against the status quo, against the dead orthodoxy of the church, against the pitiful conditions of the lower social classes. The latter attitude was out of fashion again! As though such conditions could be ignored. I found myself in a position to defend my views against formerly congenial friends . . . *Gradually Philipp and Immanuel withdrew from the Sentinel.* Subscriptions dropped to half the number. Many of these cancellations were by the clergy, my friends no longer. The turmoil strengthened me in my belief that the work of Christ and the Apostles while on earth had been built on faith in the Prophesies [sic] of the Old Testament Prophets of Israel.[32]

It's clear that, rather than developing a new Christian theology, Hoffmann adopted the teachings followed by the original Christian community – based particularly on the Gospel of Matthew – which regarded Jesus as fulfilling certain prophecies from the Old Testament. In his own words, Hoffmann observed,

these prophecies concerned mainly the founding of the *Kingdom of God* on earth. I became convinced that a revivified religion and a new social order would have to be built, one goal, one aim for the Christian. Then from several directions, mostly non-church groups, the question came: *Where should this center be located?* Since that had seemed unimportant to me, and irrelevant until then, I made a special study, to discover if a *center* were named in the prophesies [sic]. I found that some Prophets declared Jerusalem to be the center. Others mentioned Israel, that is, Palestine, to be the external manifestation of the Kingdom of God on this earth. The prophesies stress the importance of uniting and gathering God's people. This is the responsibility of those who wish to work for the salvation of mankind. There is no doubt – and I believe it with all my heart – this *Kingdom of God* has a complementary, temporal meaning as well as a spiritual one. For instance, in a Christian State, a *Kingdom of God,* the misery and famine among poor people after a crop failure is uncalled for! The Kingdom of God is a *happy state.* This is emphasised in all the Biblical prophesies,

and should exist *for all people*. The Prophets point to Jerusalem
as the Center of the Kingdom of God, a *Happy State!* Thus I
had arrived spiritually on my way to Jerusalem.[33]

By July 1852 Hoffmann was the sole editor of the *Sentinel*,
in effect alienating himself from some of his closest friends,
family and supporters as he focused his publication on his personal views and expectations. But it was at this point that a
relationship developed which was to pave the way for the carrying out of his plans, for into the picture walked the man with
whom this undertaking would be made possible, Georg David
Hardegg.

5

Brothers in Arms: Christoph Hoffmann and Georg Hardegg

Be patient, then, brothers, until the Lord's coming. See how the
farmer waits for the land to yield its valuable crop and how
patient he is for the autumn and spring rains. You too, be patient
and stand firm, because the Lord's coming is near. Don't grumble
against each other, brothers, or you will be judged. The Judge is
standing at the door!
James 5:7–9

Georg David Hardegg was born near Ludwigsberg, Württemberg, in 1812, and following a course in business studies, he found himself working in Belgium during the 1830 revolution, sparking an interest in politics which would prove to have far-reaching consequences. Two years later we find him in Paris, where he was introduced to a group of German republicans, and on returning to Württemberg in order to study medicine at Tübingen, his involvement with the political uprising led to seven years in Hohenasperg political prison, near Stuttgart, followed by several years of exile. The only reading material permitted to him in prison was the Bible, and as a result he turned to Christian mysticism, with a strongly held conviction that just as the early Christians had done, God's people would be blessed with spiritual gifts, particularly that of healing. Indeed, when he later joined with Christoph Hoffmann in gathering together God's people, this was an aspect which he was keen to pursue, although Hoffmann didn't share his conviction.

Georg Hardegg's first personal encounter with Christoph Hoffmann took place during 1849, by which time he had already supported him during the campaign against David Friedrich Strauss for a seat in the National Assembly in

Georg Hardegg   *Christoph Hoffmann*

Frankfurt in 1848 and had read his pamphlet *Voices of Prophecy regarding Babylon and God's People*. It's not clear exactly how much contact the two men enjoyed over the following years, but an historic event which took place in 1853 soon brought them together when a dispute between Russia and Turkey over the holy sites in Palestine led to war in the Crimea and the end of Turkish supremacy in Palestine; indeed, this was the opportunity Hoffmann had hoped and prayed for in fulfilling his dream of bringing together God's people in Jerusalem, and he lost no time in publishing his thoughts in the *Sentinel*.

Although Hoffmann had found in his new friend Hardegg an enthusiastic supporter of his dream for God's people, his Paulus brothers-in-law were less enthusiastic, which inevitably led to deepening division in the family. A timely invitation in 1854 to take up a position as 'Inspector of the Society of Pilgrim Missionaries' in a missionary school near Basel, Switzerland, appeared to offer Hoffmann an immediate if temporary solution to family disagreements at home, and although he accepted, it wasn't long before he became frustrated by the fact that the main focus of the school appeared to be sending missionaries out 'to convert the heathen', with apparently 'no concern for uniting and gathering the Children of God'.[1]

So it was that just ten months later he resigned his position, and although he fully expected to return with his family to either the Salon or to Korntal, the conditions required of him, which included cessation of any literary activity or work for bringing together God's people, made a return impossible; it would have meant denying what he viewed as his life's work. 'Henceforth', he stated, 'I would work for the gathering of the Children of God in Jerusalem. The Sentinel should carry my message, my call to all people who willed to hear.'[2]

His brother Wilhelm wrote with his concerns, but a more positive letter arrived from Georg Hardegg, who also arranged for the family to take up residence in Ludwigsberg. 'Good luck! Zerubabel!', he wrote, 'how happy your wife and children will be, finally to have a home! Then no more moving about from one strange residence to another, until you enter your true home in Jerusalem.'[3]

During these early beginnings of what was to become the Templer Movement the adherents were known as 'Friends of Jerusalem'. Having thrown in his lot, Georg Hardegg put all his energy into publishing the *Sentinel*, and when friends and colleagues severely criticized him for his work, Pauline reminded Hoffmann of their new friend's long years in jail as a result of his political activities in Tübingen, commenting, 'don't forget, his sweetheart remained faithful to him throughout those trying years, writing loving, encouraging letters and sending him warm knitted articles, like socks and pulse-warmers'.[4] There was no question that Hardegg's staunch character was just what Hoffmann and the movement required in moving towards its ultimate aim; 'no longer was it enough to debate questions, or discuss the probable meanings or interpretations of revelatory portions of the Bible. The time for action had come.'[5]

'Gathering of the People of God': No Going Back

The time is fulfilled, and the kingdom of God is at hand.

Mark 1:15

Although Hoffmann and Hardegg held regular meetings in Ludwigsberg which were attended by a great number of people, there was little interest in the project until, one particular evening, a small group –'less than one hundred' – stayed behind in order to find out more; 'footsteps and snatches of greetings of departing members still echoed in the empty halls, here and there a door closed noisily, as I urged these interested people to draw their chairs up closer into a more intimate circle.'

Then, as Hoffmann told his hearers that it was time 'to take practical steps', he looked into their eyes and saw 'confirmation and agreement'. He noted,

> my gaze also rested a moment upon the friends who have stood by me: G. D. Hardegg, who sat directly opposite, Christopher Paulus on his left and Louis Hoehn, Beatele's husband, on Hardegg's right side. I saw new confidence, new courage. Conscious of a renewed purpose, we formed a committee: Committee for the *Gathering of God's People in Jerusalem*. We agreed to call a public meeting and place an announcement in the Sentinel stating time and place. The ensuing meeting was well attended; friend Hardegg served as treasurer, Christopher Paulus as secretary. I was asked to preside.[1]

On 24 August 1854, about two hundred men attended an open meeting which was held in a public house in Ludwigsberg, where Hoffmann explained that in order to aid God in uniting all mankind in a perfect Christian community, the people themselves should take on responsibility for fulfilling Biblical prophecies by gathering together in Jerusalem. In late October a petition containing 439 signatures was published and sent to the National Assembly in Frankfurt, setting out the society's intention to create settlements in the Holy Land and petitioning the German Federation to consult with the Turkish Sultan in order to grant land on which to settle, as well as various rights, including religious freedom in civil and religious affairs. Although the National Assembly refused to investigate the feasibility of the project, Hoffmann and Hard-egg were unperturbed, encouraged by a membership which within just a few months had reached 500. There was no going back, despite life-changing consequences, Hoffmann declaring that

> we, in our circle, kept our standpoint no secret. It was that very autumn that Philipp Paulus, having obtained sole ownership of the 'Salon', served notice to Christopher Paulus and Louis Hoehn. He told them that their teaching assignments were terminated! Of course if these teachers should give up their interest in the Hoffmann idea of the *Gathering of the People of God,* they would be reconsidered for their positions at the Salon school.[2]

Since accommodation was included in the contract at the Salon, both families now found themselves homeless, Hoffmann and his wife, Pauline, making room in their house for the Hoehn family, and Christoph Paulus finding a house on the other side of the street.

It was at this time that Hoffmann composed the hymn *Seek ye first of all God's Kingdom,* which quickly became the theme song of the Friends of Jerusalem.[3] He also put together his *Draft of the Constitution of God's People.* His brother Wilhelm, now Court Chaplain to King Frederick William IV of Prussia, was extremely shocked by the notion of God's people gathering in Jerusalem, a utopian dream which he believed would end in disaster.

Indeed, he wasn't the only one voicing concern, the Evangelical State Church of Württemberg sending a letter from its missionary conference in May 1855 warning Hoffmann through one of its dignitaries, Prelate Sixt Karl Von Kapff, that his ideas were inaccurate, to which Hoffmann responded informing them severely that he was answerable to no-one. In the interchanges which followed, Von Kapff voiced in public his strong disapproval of the Templers, and suggested to Hoffmann that whilst hard work within the Christian community would alleviate certain problems, the situation would only change for the better with the Second Coming of Christ. Also at the missionary conference was one Pastor Volter, who accused Hoffmann and his supporters of incorrect interpretation of Biblical prophecy regarding the millennium, stressing his belief that since the bringing together of God's people lacked any Biblical evidence, the project was bound to fail.

Despite criticism and falling numbers amongst the Friends of Jerusalem, Hoffmann refused to alter his stance, berating those who denounced him for ignoring what he believed were unmistakable signs of Christ's imminent return and for allowing corruption to run its course.

In the July 1855 edition of the *Sentinel*, Hoffmann clearly stated that the purpose of bringing together God's people was to establish a lifestyle based on the word of God in order to banish the influence of dark spiritual forces in the world; he also explained that the millennium, by which was meant the conversion of the whole world, and which was the purpose of bringing together God's people, would only take place following Christ's Second Coming. However, his continuing resolution was met with dismay by the Evangelical Bishop of Jerusalem, Samuel Gobat, who declared that the curse which hung over Jerusalem would cause nothing but trials and tribulations should they carry out their plan. Hoffmann and the committee were incensed at receiving such a declaration from none other than the Bishop of Jerusalem himself, replying that they were in no way a society of dreamers, their objective merely being to establish a community based on Biblical teachings; the newly drawn-up *Constitution of God's People* was enclosed with the letter.

Then in August, Hoffmann, Hardegg and Christoph Paulus attended a Conference of the Evangelical Alliance in Paris, where they were given the opportunity to speak about their plans in front of Evangelical Christians from all over the world. Christoph Paulus gave an inspired presentation on their progress so far, reminding his audience that the Friends of Jerusalem weren't by any means the first to aspire to moving to Palestine, and bringing to mind the thousands who had emigrated to southern Russia in 1817 by way of a preparation for their onward journey to the Holy Land. Although some listened with interest, there were many who didn't, no doubt influenced by the scathing report on Hoffmann and his venture which had been written by Karl Von Kapff, who had already sown seeds of strong disapproval on several previous occasions.

However, mounting opposition failed to deter the Templer leaders from their quest to bring God's people to Palestine, and following the Paris Conference they put together a proclamation inviting Jews and Christians to support them. In October Hoffmann addressed a convention of preachers in Stuttgart, explaining in no uncertain terms that the purpose of gathering God's people in Jerusalem was in response to prophecies which named it as the starting point for the beginning of a better world. The participants weren't convinced by his persuasive arguments, their opinion no doubt influenced by a missionary who was present at the meeting, who knew Palestine well, and who believed that not only was the situation there extremely dangerous, but that the hot climate would make cultivation too difficult. But still the committee held tenaciously to their ardent belief, and no negative opinions or defeatist comments had any effect on their strong resolve.

As far as the leaders of the Friends of Jerusalem were concerned, now, more than ever, was the time to put their proposal into action, and following the advice of people who knew Palestine and its challenges, they made two important decisions: firstly, to organize a commission to Palestine in order to carry out a feasibility study; and secondly, to set up a community at home where they could equip themselves physically, mentally and spiritually for the task ahead. This focus on the situation on the home front was probably the result of strong words printed during November (1855) in the *Sentinel*, clearly pointing out that without rebirth the whole project was doomed to be unsuccessful, and reminding its readers that, inspired by the very first Christians, the focus should be purely on being a place of refuge for all those wishing to be saved.

As far as daily living and accommodation were concerned, at the beginning of the year 1856 Hoffmann, Christoph and Louis Hoehn were still living close together with their families in Ludwigsberg, Hoffmann writing that

> it was not long before we realised these arrangements were not sufficient. We should have to seek other quarters spacious enough to carry on our work. Offices and workshops would have to be separate from living quarters, which were taxed with many visitors from distances too far for justifying any in hospitality. We realized that our main, lofty purpose should not be hampered by unnecessary difficulties. We needed a station – a place where Jerusalem sojourners might gather before setting off on the distant goal. A suitable location for a group, well organised and properly instructed with a workable plan for settlement in Palestine, must be made available, to await the time when such plans would be feasible at last.[4]

The place they settled on was the Kirschenhardthof, not too far from Ludwigsberg. For several centuries the Kirschenhardthof had belonged to a large estate in Hochberg, by the Neckar river, and when Hoffmann, Hardegg and Christoph Paulus made their first visit, 'it presented a charming picture' bathed 'under a blanket of purest snow'. Its situation, complete with several cottages and outbuildings, appeared to be perfectly suited to their requirements, although when they made a second visit once the snow had thawed, they 'were appalled at the amount of renovating and repair work and cleaning up that had to be done. Immediate possession was out of the question.'⁵

The Hoffmann family were the first to move into their own cottage in April 1856; Hoffmann himself was particularly over-joyed when William Paulus and his wife Friedericke (Christoph Hoffmann's sister) joined the growing community, noting that 'William had always shown an interest in all phases of the project "Gathering the Children of God",' and adding that 'he even undertook the complicated bookkeeping system necessary for the Kirschenhardthof, it being a community affair, requiring separate records of accurate figuring for each family'. The only member still to arrive was Georg David Hardegg, who had taken a major part in the initial work, but who had some difficulty tying up his business and selling his store in Ludwigsberg:

> Whilst most of the people now at the Kirschenhardthof had grown up in small provincial towns, George David Hardegg was a city man with no experience of farm labour. He knew nothing about the frustrations of soil too wet to plough, grain flattened by rain and hail and the hay rotting in shocks, or the most important crop, potatoes, black with mold.⁶

In the autumn of 1856 Christoph Paulus established an educational institution at the Kirschenhardthof, with Herr Mueller, the headmaster from a famous girls' school in Ludwigsberg, becoming the director. Fees for children boarding at the school were high, and the pupils attending were expected to supply all clothes and bedding themselves. Christoph Paulus himself took on headship of the boys' school, with Louis Hoehn managing the public and elementary school. 'We had splendid teachers,' wrote Hoffmann, 'all the youth from the surrounding area attended the latter school.'[7]

In parallel with the school, the importance of community life was also addressed, its spiritual functioning and everyday affairs based as much as was possible on guidelines which had been laid out in the *Sentinel* earlier in the year. General instructions involving property and finances were given, as well as rules for personal conduct, with secure marriage and family being the foundation of community life. Of equal importance was the upbringing of children, which had to be based on the fear of God and disciplined hard work. Individual talents should be nurtured for the good of the whole community, and work should be balanced with social activities, which were deemed as being extremely important for community well-being. As far as was possible, daily living and tasks shouldn't be too burdensome in order to nurture both the body and mind of each individual, and the fine arts were to be given due attention both for training of the human mind and for the glory of God. To sum up, all activities were to help each individual in focusing his mind on the divine.

However, just as the community was beginning to establish its new life at the Kirschenhardthof an epidemic of typhoid fever descended on the area during the spring of 1857, raging

mostly among the children, though several adults were affected. The change from the gentler climate in Ludwigsberg to the rough winds that were nearly constant at the Kirschenhardthof region accounted for much of the suffering and distress. The nearest apothecary shop was at Marbach, where young Doctor Gottlob Paulus had his practice and extended to us every possible assistance and relief. But with the roads being impassable at times, help was not always there when most needed. It seemed almost too much to bear when Pauline and I lost our dear little Friedericke, barely 2 years old.[8]

Hoffmann himself was severely afflicted with the disease, taking several weeks to make a full recovery, and Louis Hoehn, who was not only a devoted co-worker but also Hoffmann's brother-in-law, died of dysentery. With the mail service suspended, the committee hired 'special messengers on horseback to carry manuscripts and proofs to Marbach where the Sentinel was printed. Additional messengers carried instructions *and replies* to Mr. Hardegg in Ludwigsberg.' At times the community was 'cut off entirely, waiting for the cessation of an especially heavy rain storm'. Not long afterwards sickness struck once again, with a measles epidemic which showed no mercy, Hoffmann noting, 'Pauline and I lost the baby, little Benjamin not a half year old; then seven-year-old Pauline, a beautiful child, followed. Our grief was beyond description.'[9] When the doctor suggested to Hoffmann and his family that a change of climate would aid both spiritual and physical recovery, they gratefully took his advice, returning to the Kirschenhardthof much refreshed a few weeks later.

Despite the hardships of settling into community life and a prolonged period of illness, by the end of August that year they were able to hold a series of open-air meetings on the village green, organized by Georg Hardegg, who soon proved that he 'had been endowed with a special talent for organizing and managing these and other meetings, and for classes of instruction, making him a fit leader for the actual registering of those who wished to take part in the Gathering of the Children of God'. At the meetings Hoffmann shared his future vision of the Community, which was met with criticism and accusation not only from evangelicals, particularly Pietists from Württemberg and further afield, but also from the Catholic sector. It was undoubtedly a lost cause, they claimed, and there was no doubt that it would cause misery to many impressionable souls. But there were those who were supportive, including one Herr Metz of the Metz Manufacturing Plant in Freiburg, 'whose substantial support in work and deed is just one instance of true encouragement, – there were more, some wishing to remain un-named.'[10]

Although from outside the Kirschenhardthof community appeared to be firmly united and in complete harmony, tensions between the leading members of the community soon became evident; George Hardegg's arrival on the scene as a major contributor with strong opinions of his own somewhat altered the balance regarding the way the community was organized, and although initially the situation was contained, severe ruptions later brought affairs to a head.

In the midst of this critical period with its personal and administrative tensions and life-threatening sicknesses, a pivotal decision was made, Hoffmann writing,

> During these days the words *Temple Builders* or *Temple Society* became a new designation for our movement instead of the old 'Friends of Jerusalem' - no longer was this passive term used; we now occupied a new active position. Some friends withdrew from our ranks, wanting no part of the sacrifices but only the glory that might follow. However, we gained new adherents and supporting members, and new strength. It was now possible to look forward to the actual founding of colonies in Palestine, as soon as the political situation, blocked at the moment, would make this feasible.[11]

In the meantime, when Hoffmann's brother Wilhelm suggested a visit to Berlin, the offer was gratefully accepted, including an audience with King Frederick William IV of Prussia:

> Arriving in Berlin I was graciously received at an official audience. I was given ample time to explain the great help His

Majesty's support would be to the undertaking of the Temple Society and its aim; what that would mean to us. I emphasised my staunch belief that ours was not a sentimental separatist movement, but merely a desire to carry out the responsibility of the Christian Church of Germany, it having become obscured in recent times.

However, despite the King's initial suggestion that he 'might send a commission to assist the Temple Society, if and when a survey could be undertaken to ascertain the feasibility of Christian colonies in Palestine', he was reported to have told brother Wilhelm, 'it is unthinkable that I should identify myself with these people'.[12]

During his Berlin visit Hoffmann also attended and spoke at a conference of the Evangelical Alliance, at which he rebuked the church for moving away from the spirit of Christ, for causing the current 'Babylonian' position of Christianity, and accusing it of focusing on self-righteous and irrelevant church activities. This was followed by a severe confrontation between Hoffmann and his previous adversary, Karl Von Kapff (the dignitary of the State Church of Württemberg previously referred to) at a Church Congress in Stuttgart in September 1857. The dispute carried on over the following weeks, a veritable to and fro of criticism and counter-criticism for all to read in the press, with Karl Von Kapff finally expressing his opinion that since it seemed impossible to reach agreement, he felt he should withdraw from what he deemed to be such a tiresome controversy. By this time Hardegg had entered the fray, accusing Karl Von Kapff and a few other clerics, including Hoffmann's brother-in-law Paulus, of being the main obstacle to the coming of God's Kingdom on earth due to their lack of evangelical philosophy. Having run its course without a positive outcome on either side, the confrontation shuddered to a standstill, and although the Friends of Jerusalem, now re-named the Temple Society, sensed that they had no support in educated urban circles, they were encouraged by letters in support of their venture which came not only from all over Germany, but also from Switzerland and the United States of America.

Plans for the future gained momentum, despite setbacks and criticism:

> Our funds increased more rapidly now and we were soon in a position to plan the sending of delegates to the Holy Land. A widow contributed one thousand Gulden at this time. The preparations for this preliminary journey proceeded with no further delay. Each one of these delegates would have to make arrangements for their long absence. Perhaps it would be months, even half a year, before they would return. We have not given up hope for the recovery of the King of Prussia . . . who was ill at this time, awaiting a confirmation from him for knowledgeable men to accompany us on our survey. We finally left without such assistance.[13]

Unfortunately the King's illness prevented him from offering any support to the Templers, for he was replaced by the Prince Regent, the future Emperor William 1, who exercised great caution as far as the Temple Society was concerned; however, although he wasn't prepared to offer any financial support, he did advise Prussian and Consular representatives in the Middle East to protect the commission and offered help during their fact-finding venture. Despite a few generous financial contributions, only half the required amount for the venture had been raised by the end of 1857, and believing that too much time had been lost already, the committee of the Temple Society took the decision to send only three rather than six people to Palestine, as they had originally hoped.

The three men who set off for the Holy Land on 9 February 1858, were Christoph Hoffmann, Georg David Hardegg and J. Bubeck, agriculturist and specialist in grape cultivation. At 43, Hoffmann was several years younger than his fellow travellers. 'We felt the significance of our journey deeply,' he wrote. 'Now, visibly, that is, actual steps were being taken to Gather the Children of God in Jerusalem as the central place of all Christianity, the aim and purpose of the Temple Society. This journey became a turning point in the lives of all three of us.'[14]

7

'Onward and Forward': The Scouting Tour

And I John saw the holy city, new Jerusalem, coming down from
God out of heaven,
prepared as a bride adorned for her husband.
Revelation 21: 2

Christoph Hoffman believed that the 'tour of exploration was of the greatest significance to the Temple Society'; indeed, the results were 'awaited and observed with the keenest interest as the reports came in, by the entire membership of the congregation and the readers of the Sentinel'. The party began their journey by taking the train to Berlin, where they were given official letters of introduction. A meeting with a member of the King's Cabinet produced no more than 'elaborate shoulder shrugging',[1] and although following an audience with the regent, (the King's brother, William) they received letters of recommendation to all consulates and to the ambassador in Constantinople, most of the other introductory letters were addressed to theologians who were known to be unsympathetic to both the *Sentinel* and the Temple Society.

As the journey progressed Hoffmann sent regular reports for publication in the *Sentinel* to his friend Christoph Paulus back home in Kirschenhardthof, noting that

the colourful countries and cities we passed through, and their exotic and varied customs, language, and appearance were topics that I observed now, from the viewpoint of St John's Revelations and other prophecies in the Bible. In every case, whether the town or city was large or small, it was the church and school that occupied the place of greatest prominence.

In the same passage he commented on what he regarded as the failings of the State Church, observing that

> the theoretical acceptance of the Bible by the clergy rarely took the Prophesies into account. Their views concerning these amazing portions of the Bible seemed facetious and superficial. During Bengel's time and influence in Wuerttemberg this had not been so. It was after the failure of the date 1836, set by Bengel, that his books and prophesies were also discredited almost entirely.

It appears that the articles which Hoffmann sent for publication in the *Sentinel* were met with 'enmity and bitterness', much of it directed at Hoffmann personally, although this didn't prevent him from writing further articles stressing what he considered to be the necessity for reform in the Church. 'I felt a need', he wrote, 'to impress upon the minds and hearts of the Sentinel readers the *universal purpose* of our undertaking, recounting the deeper meaning.'[2]

The journey from Berlin involved sailing by riverboat along the Elbe and Danube rivers, and then crossing the Alps on the newly constructed railway across the Semmering Pass, arriving at Trieste in 'a wild northwest wind, called *the Bora* by the natives'. The travellers managed to find their way to their ship, Hoffmann later remembering that

> we were a somber group, Bubeck, Hardegg and I, struggling with our valises and portmanteaux, hats pulled down low and collars turned up against the cold. Each one of us was sunk deep in his thoughts of home and family, yet compelled onward and forward in our mission, strengthened by our own faith, hope and aim. By God's help we were bound to succeed! I turned and nodded encouragingly to my fellow delegates, then stepped onto the gangplank and forward onto the swaying ship. A courteous cabin boy showed us through the usual mass

of weeping women and crying children, the scene of leavetak-
ing from seafaring men the world over, strangely accented by
laughter and uncomplaining good humor of ship's officers and
crew. We were hardly settled in our rather small quarters when
the obstreperous wind turned into a howling storm, the like of
which none of us had ever experienced. The brave ship headed
towards Corfu. Great rollers tossed it about in the wild sea,
causing the passages, including my two companions, to suffer
the agonies of mal-de-mer, while I remained at ease. I could
give myself over to the observation of a *storm at sea*, dramatic
and majestic – the huge waves dashing against the ship with a
shuddering power and abandon.[3]

The sea had calmed somewhat by the time the ship passed
the island of Corfu, remaining so as they voyaged onwards to
Alexandria, where they stayed for ten days. And then, at last,
the scouting party gathered at the busy harbour where they
boarded a ship bound for Jaffa, Palestine, the deck packed with

Europeans and Orientals in every type of native dress, fezes,
turbans and flowing robes, the air heavy with spicy perfumes
and odors – soon we should see the coastline of the Holy Land.
We strained our eyes on the distant horizon, fearful of missing
the first glimpse even by a moment. When land was sighted,
however, there was not much opportunity for contemplation,
for the ship dropped anchor on the far side of the breakers that
dashed against the rocks incessantly. We were met by barges
manned by powerful half-naked Arabs, chanting rhythmically
as the passengers were tossed and caught like balls in a game
with great ease and lowered with shouts of good cheer below.
The barges were then shot through the high wild waves which
were rushing across the beach. The landing place afforded the
merest shelter and barest necessities were available. Thus we set
foot upon the precious ground of Palestine. The day was 14th
of March 1858. A young man from the Pilgrim House, and

now working in Jerusalem, had been sent to meet us and help us with our luggage. He had brought horses for the two day tour from Jaffa to Jerusalem. However, we did not leave immediately, being very comfortably housed at the Jewish hostelry and in some need of rest.[4]

Keen to engage in discussion with fellow Christians at any opportunity, Hoffmann managed to have a rather frustrating conversation with the Father Superior at the Roman Catholic Monastery. After a few words on the nature of the contemplative life, Hoffmann reminded the Father that it was here, in the Holy Land, that the greater part of the revelatory chapters of the Bible had been written, to which the Father calmly responded, 'we say our prayers'. Hoffmann was disturbed to see 'no spark of interest in his face' when he reminded his listener of the importance of the Holy Land in connection with the coming Kingdom of God; 'prayers and rituals will probably drone on in near meaningless apathy for years to come,' he wrote, 'exactly as is the manner now in thousands of Christian churches of every *denomination* the world over . . .'[5]

While Hoffmann mused on the spiritual significance of the tour and engaged in deep theological conversations with Christians living in the area, his fellow travellers focused on more urgent matters, Herr Bubeck looking into agricultural possibilities in the vicinity of Jaffa, and Georg Hardegg making 'a study of Jaffa's mercantile section'. Both men were acutely aware that they were facing a culture where 'methods, traditions and customs of the land were absolutely in reversal of almost anything they had seen previously'. Hoffmann was obviously slightly perturbed as he further noted, 'how there could be any promising results at all was an enigma to my companions. They came away shaking their heads.'[6] But abandoning their quest wasn't an option, and if there were moments of alarm, they were short-lived; the three intrepid travellers had come so far, their destination was on the horizon, and moving onwards was the only conceivable option.

The journey from Jaffa to Jerusalem was made on horses, Hoffmann commenting:

> . . . the rain poured from the sky in sheets. The road was prac-
> tically non-existent and our poor beasts stumbled along the
> uphill trek coughing and snorting . . . I had not ridden a horse
> in many years and suffered from the uncomfortable saddle,
> the lashing rain, and the not unreasonable depression result-
> ing from not having a view of the country surrounding us.
> Jerusalem is situated on a plateau about 2500 feet in height, we
> were told, and some thirty miles from Jaffa. We finally halted
> at a small village asking for shelter for the night, hoping for a
> brighter outlook on the morrow. But the wind was gusty and
> rain fell intermittently even the next day, and our stony path
> was slippery in places and obliterated most of the way . . .
> Fatigued almost to exhaustion, soaked through and chilled to
> the bone, we had suddenly arrived. Dusk had fallen and the
> drizzling rain continued, so that reaching our destination at
> last – 'The Pilgrim Mission' in Jerusalem – we could hardly
> believe it. We were greeted in the friendliest manner and
> offered inexpensive hospitality for our entire stay.[7]

During his stay at the Mission House in Jerusalem Hoffmann made the acquaintance of Pastor Ludwig Schneller, who was in the process of building an orphanage and school for Arab children, and with whom he enjoyed deep discussions on Biblical texts regarding the gathering of the Children of God in Jerusalem.[8] The missionaries and workers at the Mission, however, showed no interest in the project or in Biblical prophecies, some almost to the point of disrespect and acrimony. One of them, a Pastor Valentiner,[9] even went as far as printing a formal statement in the German press in which he 'declared the plans of the Temple Society to be unfeasible'. Feeling certain that Valentiner simply misunderstood the Templer viewpoint, Hoffmann paid him a visit, only to be told in no uncertain terms that he deplored the fact that the Templer Society paid barely any attention to the Cross.[10] Christoph's response was to give a lecture setting out the aims of the Society, following which questions were

> more in the nature of heckling, rather than to express a desire to help in the reconstruction of the Church – Temple – as I called this work. Even a Bishop who was present seemed to fear for his position. – He told me later in all privacy: 'it would be impossible for me to work for the reform of the church.' His voice shook a little. 'I am kept busy justifying my position in the face of my foes in England!'[11]

Despite this apparent impasse, the Bishop eventually became supportive of the Templer movement.

Since the visit to Jerusalem was purely for gathering information, offers of property for the venture had to be declined, the small Templer group continuing their survey further afield to Bethlehem, Hebron and as far south as Beersheba 'and the dramatic region of the Jordan'. Hoffmann was keen to extend their exploration to include more remote regions which were of significance in Biblical history and therefore worthy of consideration for settlement purposes, but Hardegg viewed 'delving into the historic past as unnecessary – even feckless', telling his colleagues that their focus should be on 'investigating practical daily needs, purchasing conditions, restrictions and possibilities'; 'your intellectual pursuits have no real value', he reminded Hoffmann.[12] Finally, however, Hardegg reluctantly agreed to an extension of the tour, but with the proviso that they should travel only on well-used routes. 'My desire', wrote Hoffmann,

> consisted of the region that lies in a northeasterly direction from Jerusalem, designated in the Bible as the land where Samuel and Saul had been active. How much had these places

changed since the ancient times? Might it not be possible that this land would contain the very answer to our search? The land where the high aims and hopes of the Temple Society might be developed and prosper as examples of Christian living – could this become a reality here?

The resulting journey included Nablus, Nazareth, Akka, Haifa, (Caifa at this time), and Tiberias, the intrepid companions continuing their journey 'down a neck-breaking path, finally reaching the valley of the Sea of Merom not far from the source of the Jordan River', and leaving Palestine as they 'cut across the rugged terrain around the foot of the Mount Hermon'. On reaching Damascus they were invited to take tea with several English missionaries, who embarrassed Hoffmann by addressing his two companions as though they were merely his employees; 'but I did not correct the error,' he noted, 'fearing to exaggerate it, hoping that this mistake had not been observed by them.'[13]

On reaching Beirut Hoffmann was struck down with an attack of dysentery, although it wasn't just his health that was suffering, since relations between himself and his fellow travellers were beginning to show signs of tension; however, he noted: 'our tempers which had become quite strained and had worn thin by the unaccustomed exertions and discomforts of the sojourn through the rough regions of the country, and the intolerable heat, recovered naturally. A few days of rest worked wonders with all three of us'; so much so, it seems, that Hoffmann was able to give a sermon at the Evangelical Church, in which he stressed 'the great obligation of the Christians in the Orient and Near East to proclaim the Revelatory chapters of the Bible'.[14]

With the 'scouting' tour now complete, Hoffmann and his colleague Bubeck made arrangements for the long journey back to Württemberg. Hardegg, however, insisted that in order to do proper justice to their undertaking, they should present themselves 'at the Turkish government in Constantinople to ascertain approval from this authority for the Temple Society and their plans for settlement in Palestine'. There was much discussion on the impression it would make on the community waiting for them at Kirschenhardthof if they didn't arrive home together, Hoffmann concerned that

> this might easily be interpreted that we had quarrelled among ourselves or were not in agreement any longer. For this reason – being certain that Friend Hardegg had no selfish motive – I accompanied him as far as Smyrna, where we parted, he to proceed to Constantinople, hoping for an interview with the higher 'Gate' or Turkish authorities, while I embarked for Trieste with Herr Bubeck. With my health still in a precarious condition, I subordinated myself entirely to the wishes of the commission from this point forward. A disagreement between us undoubtably would impair the work of the Temple Society.[15]

Hoffmann was the only one to alight from the train at Kirschenhardthof: 'Herr Bubeck left the train at his own station for he was met there by his family, and naturally did not continue to the Kirschenhardthof where a large contingent from the congregation were assembled.' Unfortunately this was seen by many as being evidence of a rift between the three Templer scouts, and although this wasn't the case at that time, Herr Bubeck did withdraw from the project soon afterwards, believing that the conditions in Palestine were so appalling that 'the Temple Society's hope for *Gathering in Jerusalem* was not feasible',[16] particularly given the lack of sufficient funding. A further disappointment was that due to illness whilst in Constantinople Hardegg had failed to acquire the information he was hoping for, the uncertainty no doubt contributing to a feeling of instability in regard to the whole project.

When Hardegg finally arrived home at Kirschenhardthof he lost no time in making it his business to find fault with the management team's operation during his absence, challenging the organization and ordering changes, particularly in the running of finances, which were overseen by Wilhelm Paulus, Hoffmann's brother-in-law. From Hoffmann's perspective 'there had been nothing the least dishonest or unethical in the manner and method in which funds had been dispersed. However, the brusque questioning which Hardegg directed towards Wilhelm Paulus caused this earnest and trustworthy man to resign from his service.'[17]

Hardegg was also critical of the headmaster, Herr Mueller, who left the community and made a failed attempt at setting up a community in the Crimea. Thus, with his strongly held opinions and powerful personality, Hardegg not only got his own way concerning certain administrative changes, but also succeeded in appointing himself as secular head at Kirschenhardthof. Hoffmann was extremely upset by the way his brother-in-law, Wilhelm, had been treated but, anxious to keep the peace and protect his relationship with Hardegg, whom he still considered to be a close friend, he agreed to restrict himself to the position of spiritual leader.

Despite the difficulties, Hoffmann managed to maintain a positive outlook in regard to the overarching aim of the Temple Society, writing:

> nonetheless a milestone had been reached with our first survey journey to Jerusalem. I had set foot in the land that was to be my home. Palestine! The land we fervently hoped would be the center of the world's universal religion: *The salvation of all mankind.*[18]

8

'The Times Spoken Of in All the Prophecies': Facing the Challenge

*And He (Jesus) said to them, 'Truly I say to you, there is no one
who has left house or wife or brothers or parents or children, for
the sake of the kingdom of God, who will not receive many times
as much at this time and in the age to come, eternal life.'*
Luke 18: 29–30

An atmosphere of excitement and anticipation greeted the
three travellers on their return from the 'scouting tour', and
in order to give an in-depth report a meeting was called in the
nearby town of Cannstatt, where both Hoffmann and Hardegg
offered honest feedback on their findings. However, despite
initial optimism it soon became clear that a move to Palestine
would take longer than the committee had previously hoped,
some families in the community losing heart and deciding to
withdraw from the project altogether. Indeed, as he contemplated the amount of work which needed to be done, even
Hoffmann himself began to have serious concerns, although he
chose to dismiss them in the hope that his quest would eventually be successful. Current political events certainly served
in strengthening the resolve of both Hoffmann and Hardegg,
and they were particularly excited by the Franco-Austrian war
which commenced during the spring of 1859, and which they
viewed as being indicative of the coming apocalypse.[1]

Spurred on by his deep inner conviction, Hoffmann was
unperturbed by mounting disapproval from the Evangelical
Church authorities in Stuttgart concerning his obstinate refusal
to stop performing religious services, and their claim that only
the Church was authorized to undertake these services. But
Hoffmann no longer felt bound by church regulations, and

as a consequence his behaviour was viewed by the Consistory (church council or court) as, in effect, choosing to expel himself from the Church community. The community at Kirschenhardthof wholeheartedly supported their leader, and since they had no intention of abandoning the path which they had chosen together, they were also expelled from the church in October 1859, their objections falling on deaf ears.

As far as the Temple Society was concerned their only way forward now was to follow the path clearly shown to them in the Bible, a path which Hoffmann made absolutely clear during a meeting in February 1860 and which was attended by 400 people from all over Württemberg. It was at this meeting that the leaders of the Temple Society resolved to present a petition in person to the King, William I of Württemberg,[2] not only pleading against their expulsion from the Church, but also pointing out the hardships which both society and the Church were facing. At a further meeting held in Stuttgart in April, a deputation was formed, including both Hoffmann and Hardegg, in order to deliver the petition to the King, and despite the determined efforts of certain church officials to prevent such an audience, the King ignored their advice and even went as far as promising the delegation that he would look into some of their grievances, which unfortunately didn't happen.

A year later, in June 1861, the community members who were gathered at a meeting at the Kirschenhardthof came to the decision that they should become an independent religion, giving it the name 'German Temple'. Signed by 64 men, the document declared that

> in view of the general orientation of mankind caused by the fact that none of the existing Churches aspires to making man into a temple of God and to establish the sanctum at Jerusalem for all nations, we, the undersigned, dissociate ourselves from Babylon, that is to say from the existing Churches and Sects,

and unite to establish the German Temple, to carry out the Law, the Gospel and the Prophecy.[3]

The break from the established Evangelical Church by the Templers living at Kirschenhardthof was emulated by followers of Hoffmann living in nearby villages, who although not becoming as exclusive as those at Kirschenhardthof nevertheless formed themselves into Templer communities. This new development in the Templer movement caused outrage among the clergy of the Evangelical Church in Württemberg, who made it their business to recriminate and mock at every opportunity, with the result that the Templers not only lost basic rights such as decent funerals but also had their homes attacked. But the Templers' opinion of the Christian Church was no less damning, accusing it not only of gross misconduct but also of having abandoned the spirit of Christ's message.

Severance from the Church wasn't the only difficulty the new German Temple was faced with, as the leaders wrestled over differences of opinion, particularly in regard to the fundamental purpose of the Temple; for whilst Hoffmann believed that they should create a Christ-based community free from sinful influences coming from outside, Hardegg's view was that the focus should be entirely spiritual, with emphasis given to miracles, faith healing and prophesying, the principal task being to rebuild the Holy Land, reestablish the Temple in Jerusalem and convert the Jews. Hardegg also believed that the teaching of the sciences, or of academic subjects, was anathema to the objectives of the Temple, and although Hoffmann didn't share this view, he kept silent, believing that Hardegg's vigour and organizational skills were what would further their aims.

Difference of opinion aside, the new status of the German Temple required organization, with Hoffmann taking the position of Bishop and Hardegg overseeing the committee in charge of establishing of the Temple in Jerusalem. Hardegg also set up a 'School for Prophets' in order to educate young men in the fundamental tenets of the Temple, with missionaries being dispatched as far as Palestine, Russia and America, where people were already aware of Templer religious concepts through reading the *Sentinel*. A few young volunteers from Kirschenhardthof who were sent off to the Schneller orphanage in Jerusalem in order to learn Arabic had hoped to settle in Palestine, but feeling that such a move was premature, the Temple committee advised against it.

In the midst of dealing with organization and coping with difficult relationships during the early 1860s, personal life at home still had challenges which were hard to bear, Hoffmann and his wife Pauline losing three more children in as many years. Making ends meet was also challenging, Hoffmann supplementing his meagre income by 'giving a series of lectures on various philosophic subjects in the city of Ludwigsburg', and although his lectures were well attended and rewarding, 'the long three hour walk during the rough winter season brought on a severe throat ailment that had to be operated on eventually'.[4]

During the year 1862 attempts were made by the leading Templers to gain the support of what they hoped would become a politically united Germany, but the Pan-German party, whose own remit was to unify all of Germany, rejected any suggestions from the Templers of integrating political and religious concepts, and so their attempt failed. And then, when in 1866 the Austro-Prussian War, (the Seven Weeks' War), came 'over Germany like a sudden thunderstorm' and disappeared 'just as fast', Hoffmann noted that he and his fellow Templers saw it as 'another sign from heaven for us to set out soon for Palestine. We felt with a new impact and certainty how the governments, evilly advised, have no compunction whatever, but selfishly destroy the life and goods of the masses of people.'[5]

Unfortunately the year 1866 also brought with it renewed divisions between Hardegg and Hoffmann concerning the practice of spiritual healing, coming to a head when a young girl who claimed to be 'obsessed', and who apparently received spiritual revelations, was proved by Hoffmann to be a fraud. Hardegg was reluctant to admit that he had been taken in, and since Hoffmann was unwilling to mortify his colleague, he allowed the mistake to pass by without comment; however, despite Hoffmann's attempt to improve the situation, the incident only served to humiliate Hardegg and to deepen further a growing sense of mistrust between the two men.

The ultimate aim of the German Templers was still to 'gather the Children of God in Jerusalem as the central place of all Christianity',[6] and despite ongoing difficulties in ensuring its success plus personal tensions at home in the community, both Hoffmann and Hardegg nevertheless held out hope for its eventual success. But they weren't the only Christians with such plans, for in the autumn of 1866 a group of 156 Americans calling themselves 'The Church of Messiah', with their leader George Jones Adams, landed at the port in Jaffa, complete with building materials and farming equipment, their hope being that in assisting the return of the Jewish people to the Holy Land this would hasten the return of the Messiah.[7] Despite their best intentions however, by December 1867 conditions and circumstances proved too difficult for the American settlers to overcome, and with their hopes dashed, all but 20 of the group returned home.

It was in 1867 that Hoffmann wrote of his dismay concerning a group of Templers who 'expressed their impatience by moving prematurely to settle in Palestine, not waiting for a consultation with us at the Kirschenhardthof. Because of their ignorance of conditions and lack of knowledge of the language, they suffered and endured great hardship. They built homes and maintained themselves on small farms . . . just barely surviving . . . on the western slope of the hills near Nazareth.' Others followed shortly afterwards, Hoffmann noting that young men in the Templer community at home in Germany who were of military age and who 'could not condone certain aggressive moves of the government' were also keen to 'leave for the Holy Land without delay'.[8] Indeed, some were so impatient to move away that they left for America and Russia, despite pleas from the Templer leaders to be patient.

Unfortunately the Templer leaders felt unable to recognize or support the settlement near Nazareth, Hardegg eventually going as far as expelling them from the Society altogether, despite their desperate living conditions, severe illnesses and several deaths. Hoffmann later wrote,

> until now I had not imagined the Unification *of Christians* and the Gathering of the Children of God in Jerusalem to consist of these small, insignificant groups of immigrants. My chief hopes were based on an idea of a closely knit spiritual understanding permeating thoroughly a vast assembly of Christians. These Children of God – Templers – well able to maintain themselves independently would have one aim: reclaiming, restoring, rebuilding, and re-spiritualizing the church until the times spoken of in all the Prophesies of the Bible.[9]

It was towards the beginning of this crucial period that the founder of the Red Cross, Henri Dunant, was involved in creating an international society for the development of trade, industry and agriculture in the Middle East, with a particular focus on Palestine. Since Europe didn't appear to show any interest in the project, the leaders of the German Temple, inspired by his idea, decided to present a petition to Austria, England, Italy, France, North America, Prussia and Russia, at the same time setting up a temporary mission station in Palestine. Within a month Hardegg had come up with a draft petition entitled 'The Oriental Question in the Light of Prophecy', shortly afterwards travelling to Paris in order to meet Henri Dunant, who at the time happened to be the chairman of the International Society for Palestine. Through some successful consultation Dunant's International Society agreed to mediate between the Turkish government and the Templers in negotiations related to land purchase, Dunant expressing nothing but praise to Hardegg and the Temple Society for being among the first to be part of such a potentially fruitful biblical undertaking. Unfortunately, although the Templers gave Dunant substantial funds for his work on their behalf, he lost his entire wealth in a failed agricultural project in Algiers, not only failing to gain a permit for land purchase from the Ottoman government, but also unable to return the funds he had been advanced.

Despite their growing differences of opinion, having observed the failure of both the 'The Church of Messiah' and the unofficial Templer settlement near Nazareth, Hoffmann and Hardegg agreed that the only way their long-term plans for settlement in Palestine would succeed was with meticulous planning and organization. With this in mind a meeting was held in February 1868 at which the Elders of the Society set up a settlement fund; and at a further meeting at the Kirschenhardthof in March Nazareth was selected as being the first official Templer settlement in Palestine, with Hoffmann appointed as the Elder in charge, and prepared, along with his family, to emigrate without further delay. Since Hardegg and his family were ready to join them, plans were made for the first group of Templers to leave for Palestine on Thursday, 6 August 1868.

As the two families prepared for their departure, a great deal of forward planning was set in motion, whilst at home some reorganization was put in place so that the Society would run smoothly following their departure, with Christoph Paulus appointed as Head of the Temple Society in Germany and editor of the *Sentinel*. However, as preparations were under way Hoffmann began having second thoughts regarding the timing of their project, remembering in particular the crises two years earlier when his already fragile relationship with colleague Hardegg had been severely tested by the scandal in relation to spiritual healing, and which had been brought to a head by a young girl claiming to be 'obsessed'.

Hoffmann's immediate solution was to delay his departure and allow Hardegg to go ahead without him. However, when Hardegg merely shrugged off their differences and the Temple leaders expressed their fear that without Hoffmann the whole project would be put at risk, he rescinded, and a grand farewell meeting was arranged at the Kirschenhardthof towards the end of July, attended by 1,200–1,500 fellow Templers and friends.

9

'Gratitude and hope':
Fulfilling the dream

. . .the splendour of Carmel and Sharon; they shall see the glory of
the Lord,
and the excellency of our God.
Isaiah 35:2

Christoph Hoffmann's dream was finally about to be fulfilled
as the small company of Templers took leave of their home
in Germany for the final time. He later wrote of their departure, 'Friend Hardegg and I with our families and belongings
were on our way to establish permanent homes in Palestine.
We had said our farewells and the train pulled out of Ludwigsburg.' There were a few further farewells to be made along
their journey, beginning with Hoffmann's son, Samuel, who
was studying medicine in Tübingen and who met them briefly
at Noerdlingen station 'for the handclasp exchange of good
wishes. Pauline, pleased to see him, managed a smile and I said
a few words of encouragement; too soon, our train moved out
and away.'

Further along their route they took a steamer to Vienna,
which 'made a pleasant change and was done to please our
young ladies'. Having stopped at Budapest in order to meet
friends, their journey continued 'under pleasant weather conditions on the beautiful Danube for several days through the
remainder of Hungary and Serbia as far as the *Iron Gate of*
Turkey at Ruschtschuk'[1] where they spent the night at an inn
named the *City of London*. On reaching Varna, on the coast of
Bulgaria, they waited for the Austrian steamer to take them
across the 'tumultuous Black Sea. We had obtained a cabin
for our ladies, but the men of our party remained on deck,

sleeping on pallets, and found what rest we might at night. We were travelling third class, naturally, to conserve our funds as much as we possibly could.'²

Hoffmann's son Christoph, who worked at Hardegg's Mercantile Establishment in Odessa, had travelled the 829 kilometres to Constantinople (Istanbul) in order to see his parents as they passed through, and as soon as their steamer dropped anchor he joined them on board, Hoffmann noting with great relief that he came 'with a few carriers to help us through all the difficulties of landing'. During their stay in Constantinople both Hoffmann and Hardegg, along with their families, were invited to stay at the home of Messud Bey, a high-ranking Turkish official of Belgian descent, which according to Hoffmann was a

> most satisfactory arrangement; he was delighted with our European cookery and we with the comfortable living quarters – a friendly exchange that pleased us all. The house was in the Pera Heights district, lying especially convenient for us to attend to our countless business and official transactions, which we were obliged to accomplish with the Turkish government before proceeding to our destination.³

It was during their stay in Constantinople that Hoffmann and Hardegg made efforts to acquire permission from the Turkish Government for a lease, with the possibility of purchase, on some land on Mount Carmel, in Haifa; however, despite the help of the North German Federation, no decision was come by, and the Templer party travelled on towards their destination with the matter unresolved.

With the end of their journey in sight and settlement now just a matter of days away, Hoffmann noted,

> our experience on our first visit to Jerusalem accounted for the decision not to settle within that city, but locate outside

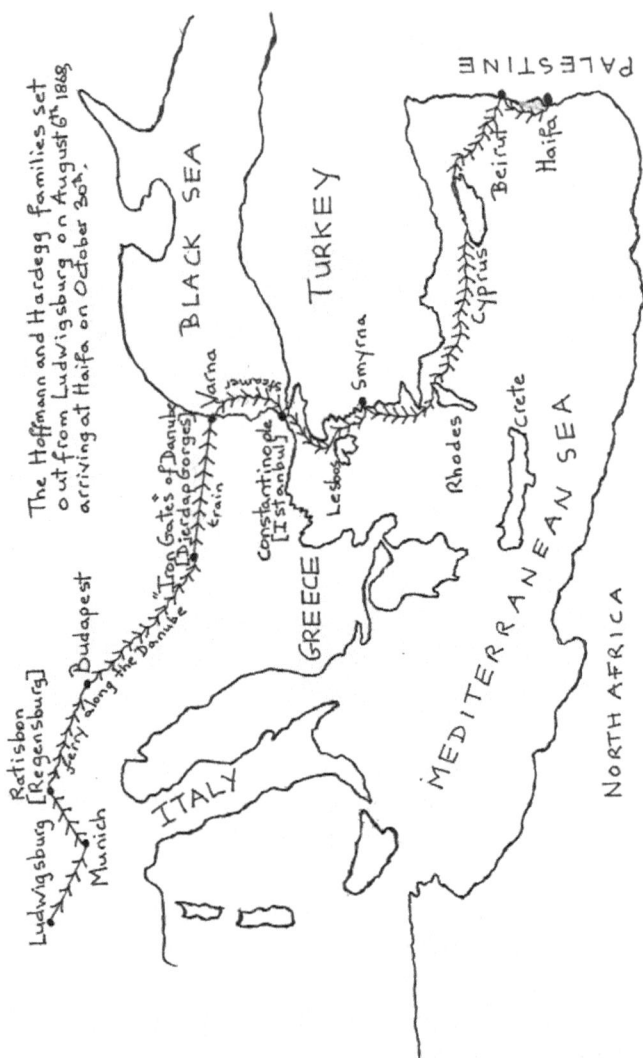

The Hoffmann and Hardegg families set out from Ludwigsburg on August 6th 1868, arriving at Haifa on October 30th.

PALESTINE

Beirut

Haifa

BLACK SEA

TURKEY

Cyprus

Varna

Danube

Constantinople [Istanbul]

Smyrna

Lesbos

Rhodes

Crete

"Iron Gates of Danube [Djerdap Gorges]
train

Budapest

ferry along the Danube

Ludwigsburg [Regensburg]
Ratisbon

Munich

GREECE

ITALY

MEDITERRANEAN SEA

NORTH AFRICA

in the open country. The many contrasting factions already occupying space within Jerusalem, we feared might curtail our freedom of action and cause additional difficulties. The exact location unknown as yet would certainly be enhanced if it were secluded rather than too near the constant traffic of the thoroughfare. We hoped to find such a place near Nazareth. On our first Palestine journey we had met a Reverend Huber engaged by an English mission in that vicinity, who had given us much information that made Nazareth sound advantageous at that time. Reverend Huber had visited us in return at the Kirschenhardthof, where he stayed with us for a month or more finding much of our philosophy and Bible interpretation in agreement with his own. I wrote him from Constantinople to tell him of our approaching arrival in Palestine. His answer was most friendly and sincere, expressing his desire to be of service to the Templers when we arrived.[4]

In mid-October the party left Constantinople for Beirut, where they met up with a group of Templers who had recently arrived from Russia, and where Hardegg had organized some meetings which Hoffmann believed 'could not be disregarded'; 'this suited me very well', he further commented, 'for I was anxious to check some of my new ideas about the vicinity of Nazareth.'[5] However, following some advice from people with knowledge and experience, Hoffmann realized how important it was to choose their first site wisely, noting,

I was greatly perturbed when Dr Weber[6] advised against the idea of choosing the vicinity of Nazareth for our first settlement. 'It is too far removed from civilisation!' he exclaimed. At the same time an urgent letter reached us from the young missionary Huber with whom we had previously corresponded. He gave us reasons why Caifa – later called Haifa – would be much more suitable for location of the first Temple Society colony than Nazareth, contrary to his former view. It seemed

to him that the advantages of Haifa outweighed anything that
Nazareth might offer. He mentioned especially the harbour
and shipping of Haifa as well as the postal connections . . . The
decision was now made to settle at the coast city of Haifa with
its reputation for a delightful climate. To our great surprise we
learned upon docking at Haifa that two Templer families had
followed us from Germany reaching the city long in advance.
They had actually started negotiations for renting or leasing
homes for us, but unfortunately were out of town on the day of
arrival, we were informed by a messenger from the Consulate.
We learned that these two families who had followed us, inves-
tigated the environs of Nazareth immediately upon their arrival
and, finding conditions according to the later report received
from missionary Huber, decided against settling there.[7]

Arrangements were made by the Consulate for the Hoffmann
and Hardegg families to stay temporarily in some 'small huts'
belonging to a Russian couple who had provided them for the
use of the hundreds of Russian pilgrims who visited Jerusalem
during Christmas and Easter holidays. Hoffmann noted that

the facilities were modest but adequate, and our kind hosts
soon had a samovar going, serving us hot aromatic tea. Seldom,
we declared, had ever a cup of tea tasted better – it was a welcome warm with friendship. There were steaming plates of
vegetable soup – borscht – too, with chunks of nourishing
black bread. We sat on benches around a long wooden table in
a separate building – just as our hosts were accustomed to serving the pilgrims. Their good natured friendliness cheered us as
much as the meal. The first storm of the winter season broke
towards morning. It obliged us to remain in our pilgrim abodes
for an entire week, or eight days . . . Not one of us thought
of complaining or grumbling – not even the children, neither
about the weather nor the very small quarters where we were
crowded like sheep. Gratitude and hope swelled our hearts,

and our spirits were filled with praise for the goodness of God, that we had arrived – not only safely – but ahead of this storm.[8]

Not long after the first Templers arrived in Haifa and began planning the building of their first settlement, the American writer Mark Twain penned an account of his travels through Europe and the Holy Land in his 1869 book, *The Innocents Abroad*, leaving a memorable description of his impression:

> Of all the lands there are for dismal scenery, I think Palestine must be the prince. The hills are barren, they are dull of color, they are unpicturesque in shape. The valleys are unsightly deserts fringed with a feeble vegetation that has an expression about it of being soulful and despondent . . . It is a hopeless, dreary, heartbroken land . . . Palestine is desolate and unlovely . . . [9]

If Hoffmann and Hardegg viewed their new home with similar pessimism, they were too preoccupied to dwell on such things, focusing, instead, on the enormous task ahead of them.

By the spring of 1869 land had been acquired on the outskirts of Haifa which was suitable for a permanent settlement, and shortly afterwards Hoffmann noted that they were joined by Templers who had previously journeyed to Nazareth from Germany without sufficient funds and against all advice. 'They arrived at the door of our cabin thoroughly soaked, emaciated, and downcast from the sickness and deaths that had occurred among them during the last year,' he wrote.

> We absorbed them in our group, helping them and sharing with them to the best of our ability and means. The situation required action: testing of our faith. I marvelled at how this experience brought forth a true understanding of the Templer aims. It helped us seek the work that lay before us, giving us an enlightened vision of the meaning of Gathering the Children of God in Jerusalem.[10]

The longed-for dream, the supreme mission of the Temple Society was at last becoming a reality.

In addition to the business of establishing homes and work in Haifa, the small Templer community now had to make a decision concerning the question of overall leadership. Having agreed to establish their first centre in Haifa by way of a base for further settlements elsewhere in Palestine, Hardegg made it quite clear that he wished to have complete control of the project, and his domineering manner had already shown that he wasn't amenable to quiet consultation. As tensions between the two leaders escalated, Hoffmann realized that living within the same close community would soon become untenable; and so when in March 1869 the possibility arose of moving south to the town of Jaffa, he viewed it as an opportunity not only of relieving the present problem, but also a way of founding a second Templer community, which he was able to do by buying property which had belonged to the failed American colony, the Church of the Messiah.

Despite their widening differences, the two leaders nevertheless agreed on the vital question of who, and how many members of the Temple Society should be encouraged to emigrate to Palestine. Having taken the momentous step themselves and seen first hand the extreme challenges which such a move entailed, their concern now was that future emigrants should fulfil certain requirements, such as having specific skills and a means of support. By 1870 a rule had been established whereby the Templer committee back home in Württemberg only allowed members to emigrate if they had received a specific request from Palestine, and although this did restrict the number of settlers, it assured a degree of economic stability.

Mass emigration, therefore, was out of the question, and Hoffmann was prepared to expel any Templers who undertook the move without first of all going through rigorous planning and vetting. This greatly upset many Templers at home in Germany whose sole purpose was emigration to Palestine, and as a result, many left the Society. Hoffmann and Hardegg were in agreement on this matter, however, and Hoffmann was unshaken in his abiding conviction that his vision of the future gleaned from his study of biblical prophecy was correct; he also believed that it was of the utmost importance to take into account the economic and social realities of the project, without which his vision for a new society based on true Christian spirit would inevitably fail.

Hoffmann's new venture in Jaffa, the extension of the Society into new colonies elsewhere in Palestine, and the often complicated and painful history of the Templers over the coming decades are addressed in the Epilogue. In focusing on the history of the Templer colony in Haifa, where Hardegg struggled to establish and maintain his authority, we will now take a glimpse at the fascinating and significant relationship which developed between the Templers and a few members of the small Bahá'í community also living in Haifa, and more importantly, with their leader living in the prison city of Akka just a few miles across the bay.

10

'Could the Signs of the Times be Clearer?': A Meeting of Minds

But of that day and hour knoweth no man, no, not the angels of heaven,
but my Father only.
Matthew 24:36

In 1869, a Templer architect by the name of Jakob Schumacher arrived in Haifa with his family from Ohio, United States, and it was to him that Hardegg turned in order to draw up plans for the new colony, using Hardegg's own specifications. Soon after Schumacher's arrival construction began for the first four Templer homes in Haifa, with the foundation stone of the Community Hall being laid on 23 September. The area chosen as the ideal situation for the new settlement lay to the west of the old walled town, between the Mediterranean Sea and the foot of Mount Carmel, with the houses lining both sides of a new street which at the time was given the name Karmelstrasse, and later renamed Ben Gurion Avenue. By 1873 the settlement in Haifa had at its disposal 38 dwellings, and had grown to a community of 250 inhabitants.

During the first few years attempts to establish vineyards on the slopes of Mount Carmel were hampered by poor soil, and even basic agriculture and cattle breeding proved to be extremely challenging; although determined perseverance eventually produced some results despite the poor soil, many settlers decided to focus instead on construction and trade, which proved to be far more lucrative. However, it was when they turned their attention to transport that the settlers really began to reap financial benefits aplenty. Before their arrival in Palestine the carriage[1] as a means of transport was virtually unknown, and the Templer settlers lost no time in establishing

Views of the Templer settlement in Haifa

a successful business not only in goods transport but also for passengers, providing a regular service between Haifa and Akka, at the northern end of Haifa Bay. They were also instrumental in an initiative to improve the rough track between Haifa and Nazareth, constructing a road which was capable of taking horse-drawn vehicles. In the centre of the settlement in Haifa they built a European-style guest house, the Karmel hotel, and as their transport and tourist initiatives gradually expanded over the following decades, their efforts successfully contributed to a growing tourist industry in Palestine.

It was during this early period of the new venture that a further, smaller settlement was started just outside the city walls in Jerusalem, and that Hoffmann's brother-in-law, Christoph Paulus, joined the steady stream of Templers leaving Germany for Palestine. From all appearances, the future seemed extremely promising for all those dedicated to the cause.

On 29 June 1871 an article written by Schumacher appeared in the *Sentinel* (still the German Templer magazine), in which he wrote about the group of Bahá'ís who had arrived in Palestine two months before Hoffmann and Hardegg in 1868:

I can give notice of yet another spiritual phenomenon which can strengthen our belief. This concerns 70 Persians, who have been banished to Akka on account of their beliefs. Mr Hardegg has already spent considerable time and effort trying to discover the actual basis of their belief, and had dealings with them through an interpreter just yesterday. He has found that this people base themselves on the Holy Scriptures and, like us, are awaiting the hour of Redemption in God's Kingdom. The home of this movement is the Persian border-country near Baghdad. The greater part of these Persian friends of the Bible are still to be found in their homeland. Since the Shah was unable to suppress the movement, he has taken captive the leaders and sent them into exile ever further from their homeland until they finally arrived in Akka. These people have

The Karmel hotel

endured the ordeals and agonies of the first Christians, have no connections with any European missionary society and live the simple Bible beliefs untouched by European influence . . . Could the signs of the times be clearer? What more could happen to show us what times we are living in?[2]

A few weeks later, on 20 July, a further article appeared in the *Sentinel*, this time written by Hardegg himself, who had obviously lost no time in making contact with the few Bahá'ís who had established themselves in Haifa:

In the town of Haifa by Carmel live a few Persians, who earn their living as metal and wood-workers. They stand out on account of their sensible and friendly faces and their Persian dress. They are members of a Persian sect, the leader and members of which, together with wives, children and servants, to the number of about 80 souls, are confined by the Ottoman Government to Akka, three hours from here. An acquaintance sprung up between myself and these persons in Haifa and, in the course of our exchanges, I received the impression that these people, despite all the obscurity of their knowledge, were seeking truth.

In order to be more accurately informed, I sought an interview with the leader, Bahá'u'lláh, which may be translated as 'the Light or Illuminer of God'; his family name is Nuri, formerly large landowners in Persia. The interview took place on 2 June in Akka with the son of Bahá'u'lláh, 'Abbás Effendi, a man of twenty-seven years, one of the educated inhabitants of Akka acting as interpreter.

I opened by saying to 'Abbás Effendi that if my communication with him would bring about difficulties with the authorities, I would leave it to his discretion to discontinue. To this he replied: in Persian there is a saying: beyond black, there is no other colour, i.e. after so much suffering it could hardly become worse.[3]

It's clear that Hardegg had made contact with the Bahá'ís living in Haifa very soon after his own arrival, and that through this contact he was made aware of the Bahá'ís living as prisoners across the bay in the prison city of Akka. Indeed, Bahá'u'lláh Himself addressed a letter to Hardegg some time in 1871, and by July 1872 this letter, or Tablet,[4] had been roughly translated and sent to the English Church Missionary Society by the Reverend John Zeller, who originally came from Württemberg, and who, with James Huber, was a missionary in Nazareth. Zeller's letter accompanying the Tablet was dated 8 July 1872. In his Annual Letter dated 28 November 1872, Huber described a visit which he made with Hardegg to Akka in order to meet with the Bahá'ís there:

One cannot say, that the Mohammedans are unwilling to listen to religious conversations, and especially Europeans are treated with civility. They also know the difference between evangelical Christianity, and that of the Eastern Churches which they cannot esteem very highly.

About a month ago, I had occasion to see some of the Persian 'Baabys' at Akka. As the Germans have a colony at Caiffa, which being about nine miles distant, some of the Persians came several times to Mr Hardegg, the head man of the colony, and he thought that they that are anxious to learn something about Christianity, but he could never exactly ascertain their real desire, and as they invited him, and promised him an interview with their Prophet, 'Behau Allah' (Lustre of God) Mr Hardegg wrote to me, inviting me to join him. I informed Mr Zeller about it, and he thought it also interesting and told me to go. From Caiffa we went early in the morning and arrived at Akka at 8 o'clock. We went on a carriage kept by the German Colonists which being a great improvement and a pleasure to every one who wishes for the spiritual and temporal welfare of this country.

After we had rested a little we went to the house where 'Behau Allah' and his son, Abbas Effendi are living and watched by some Turkish police-men. After some conversation we found out that it is not their wish to bring us near their Prophet, and all possible excuses were made why we could not see him and converse with him. We then began to speak to Abbas Effendi about the miserable state of fallen mankind; the necessity of a Redeemer; and how it was our duty to do something for our own salvation, and for that of our fellow men; especially those who were considered heads of a religious sect aught to employ their time in that way, etc. Abbas Effendi, like the Druses, agreed to all we said, and seemed very well informed; but he thought it necessary to learn some of the European languages well, in order to be able to converse with Europeans in their own language. We told him, that there was more important work to do for spiritual men. The wisdom of this world seems to be to them more than the simple faith in Christ and his

SEEKING A STATE OF HEAVEN

word, as they are too wise in their own imagination. I think they are seeking for the protection of a European Power and for nothing else. It may be, that, if there was a missionary at Akka, who could see them often some of them might be led to the truth and knowledge of Christ.[5]

Zeller too referred to his contact with the Bahá'ís living in Akka in his Annual Letter of December 1872, and was eventually successful in meeting 'Abdu'l-Bahá in 1874. Although Georg Hardegg met with 'Abdu'l-Bahá, his ultimate hope of obtaining a meeting with Bahá'u'lláh Himself never materialized, Bahá'u'lláh alluding to it in a Tablet addressed to a Bahá'í living in Haifa sometime around the year 1875. In the Tablet Bahá'u'lláh refers not only to the fact that the appearance of the Promised One in the Holy Land is mentioned in all the Holy Books, but also that the Templers had travelled from far away in order to live in that very same Holy Land. Reference is made to an inscription over one of the doors in the Templer Colony in Haifa, namely, '*Der Herr ist nahe* [The Lord is nigh] *1871*' to which the Templers were reported to have responded, '*Zuhúr nazdík ast . . .*The theophany [manifestation] is nigh and we have come that we might attain unto it (his presence).' However, despite their apparent understanding of the times they were living in, Bahá'u'lláh pointed out that they remained in a state of heedlessness. Finally, reference is made to Hardegg's failed attempt to meet Bahá'u'lláh, to the Tablet which Bahá'u'lláh addressed to him, and to the fact that despite clearly being shown the way to true salvation, no one was able to attain to 'even a drop of the ocean of its significances'.[6]

Given that any communication or meeting between the Templers and the Bahá'ís was dependent on an interpreter, the potential for true understanding was extremely limited, particularly in view of the fact that at the time none of Bahá'u'lláh's Writings had been translated from their original Arabic or Persian into German. It's clear, then, that given the limitations of

their encounters, the Templers were unaware of the true significance of Bahá'u'lláh's message, particularly in relation to their
own mission. Who, then, was Bahá'u'lláh, and what exactly
was His message? A clue is to be found in an important letter
which He penned in 1868, and in which He addressed the
Christians of the world, clearly setting out the nature of His
Mission and referring to His pen as His 'most mighty Trumpet,
whose blast is to signalize the resurrection of all mankind'.[7]

Bahá'u'lláh's claim was, in fact, nothing less than that He fulfilled the prophecies pertaining to the 'end times' in both the
Old and New Testaments of the Bible and in all major Faiths.
Thus, for Christians He was the return of Christ, the longed-
for Second Coming. 'The time foreordained unto the peoples
and kindreds of the earth is now come,' He proclaimed:

> The promises of God, as recorded in the holy Scriptures, have
> all been fulfilled. Out of Zion hath gone forth the Law of God,
> and Jerusalem, and the hills and land thereof, are filled with
> the glory of His Revelation. Happy is the man that pondereth
> in his heart that which hath been revealed in the Books of God
> . . .[8]

And again He stated, specifically addressing the Christians:

> We, in truth, have opened unto you the gates of the Kingdom
> . . . He, verily, hath again come down from heaven, even as He
> came down from it the first time . . .
>   . . . Say, Lo! The Father is come, and that which ye were
> promised in the Kingdom is fulfilled! This is the Word which
> the Son concealed, when to those around Him He said: 'Ye
> cannot bear it now.' And when the appointed time was fulfilled
> and the Hour had struck, the Word shone forth above the hori-
> zon of the Will of God. Beware, O followers of the Son, that
> ye cast it not behind your backs. Take ye fast hold of it. Better
> is this for you than all that ye possess. Verily He is nigh unto

them that do good. The Hour which We had concealed from the knowledge of the peoples of the earth and of the favoured angels hath come to pass. Say, verily, He (Jesus) hath testified of Me, and I do testify of Him. Indeed, He hath purposed no one other than Me. Unto this beareth witness every fair-minded and understanding soul.[9]

It's not entirely clear to what extent Georg Hardegg and his fellow Templers were made aware of this monumental affirmation, although the probability is that given their strong conviction regarding their own mission in Palestine, and their hope of converting the Bahá'ís to Christianity, their minds wouldn't have been able to contemplate Bahá'u'lláh's claim. Despite the difficulties in communication and difference in basic belief, however, the Templers and the Bahá'ís were certainly respectful of each other, which became evident when Bahá'u'lláh later spent some time staying in a Templer house at the foot of Mount Carmel.

Despite the stimulating communications and visits which Hardegg pursued with the Bahá'ís in Haifa and in Akka during the early years of the new colony, life within the colony itself wasn't always straightforward, for as tensions between Hoffmann and Hardegg intensified, so too did those within the nascent community in Haifa, despite its rapid and successful development for which Hardegg was undoubtedly responsible. Indeed, his plans for the colony were extremely ambitious, and with his colleague Hoffmann safely installed in the Jaffa colony a hundred kilometres away, he was able to forge ahead with little or no consultation; as a result the Central Council in Germany decided to withdraw funding from the Haifa community, which by 1874 was unable to function at all. The more recent members of the Haifa colony found Hardegg's dictatorial leadership hard to live with, and his apparent wish to become overall head of the Templer movement no doubt added to their disquiet.

In an attempt at reconciliation the Haifa community decided to share their concerns with Hoffmann, who from the safe distance of his own community in Jaffa stated that the only solution he would consider was Hardegg's resignation, which Hardegg implemented on 31 March 1874, simultaneously withdrawing his membership of the Temple Society and taking about a third of the Haifa community with him. Despite the growing disagreements and a deepening conflict in spiritual conviction between the two leaders of the project in Palestine, this was doubtless an extremely difficult moment for Hardegg, for whom the Templer cause had been his overriding passion for 20 years. His place as head of the Temple Society in Haifa was taken over by the architect Jakob Schumacher,[10] and it was under his devoted leadership and that of his successor, Friedrich Lange, that the Templer community in Haifa was rejuvenated.

Hardegg and those who left the Templer Society with him tried to join, firstly, the Lutheran Church of Sweden and secondly, the Anglican Church Missionary Society, both of whom refused them. In 1878 Hardegg formed his own Temple Association, but when he died a year later it dwindled. Eventually those followers who remained were persuaded to join the Evangelical State Church of Prussia. Hardegg died in July 1879 and is buried in the Templer cemetery in Haifa.

11

'These Doors Shall Be Opened': An Uncertain Future

I am the Alpha and the Omega, the First and the Last,
the Beginning and the End.
Revelation 22:13

Following Hardegg's withdrawal and subsequent death, Hoffmann continued to be the spiritual leader of the Templer community in Jaffa. By this time there were four Templer communities in Palestine, namely Jaffa, Haifa, Jerusalem and Sarona, near Jaffa, all of which were now taken care of by one supreme council. As far as making a living and establishing themselves in their communities was concerned, their main focus was on farming, for which they used modern working techniques such as steam-powered mills and oil presses, which until that time were unknown in Palestine. They also produced soap and cement, introduced pharmacies and hotels, made Sarona famous for the Jaffa orange, and contributed a distinctive architecture to their new districts with beautiful European-style homes. However, with dwindling support from the German homeland during the mid-1870s and a resulting drop in the number of members willing to consider emigration to Palestine, Hoffmann decided to return to Germany in order to stimulate interest and commitment. Stuttgart was by this time the centre of the German Temple, and it was from here that for 18 months Hoffmann spread the word on the project in Palestine through lectures and conferences.

Hoffmann had no doubt at all that the headquarters of the Templer Society should ultimately be in Jerusalem, which he still considered as being the main focus as far as religious expectations were concerned; however, economic circumstances had so far prevented this plan from materializing. On returning from his trip to Germany he made the decision that the time was now ripe for such a move, and any misgivings he had were overridden by his conviction that the Society would eventually fail if it didn't transfer its headquarters to Jerusalem, the true and only spiritual centre. The move took place early in 1878 with funds contributed by some wealthy Templers who had been persuaded by Hoffmann of the importance of spiritual sacrifice, and almost 100 camels were used for the task of transporting all the furniture, personal possessions and people from Jaffa to Jerusalem.

Shortly before the move, Hoffmann took steps to protect the Templer movement from reverting to old church doctrine by forming a theological institute, or *Tempelstift*, a community of people whose spiritual focus was on personal, family and social life, and the concept of striving to establish God's Kingdom on earth.

Whereas previously he had respected the sacraments of baptism and holy communion, he now deliberately made a point of separating the Temple Society from the established Church once and for all, claiming that the sacraments of baptism and communion, as well as the doctrine of the Holy Trinity, were to be found nowhere in the Bible; he even went as far as to say that the doctrine of the Holy Trinity was ridiculous. Hoffmann spread his views widely through three letters, with the result that a great deal of discussion went on not only amongst the Templer community, but also outside, including the *Tempelverein* (Temple Association) which Hardegg had established, and which fiercely upheld the Christian doctrine of the Lutheran Church as well as gifts of the Holy Spirit, without which Hardegg believed the Temple dream would never be possible. When Hardegg died in 1879 the majority of his supporters returned to the Protestant Church.

In 1880 a group of Templers, including Christoph Paulus, undertook a busy lecture and conference tour to the Templer

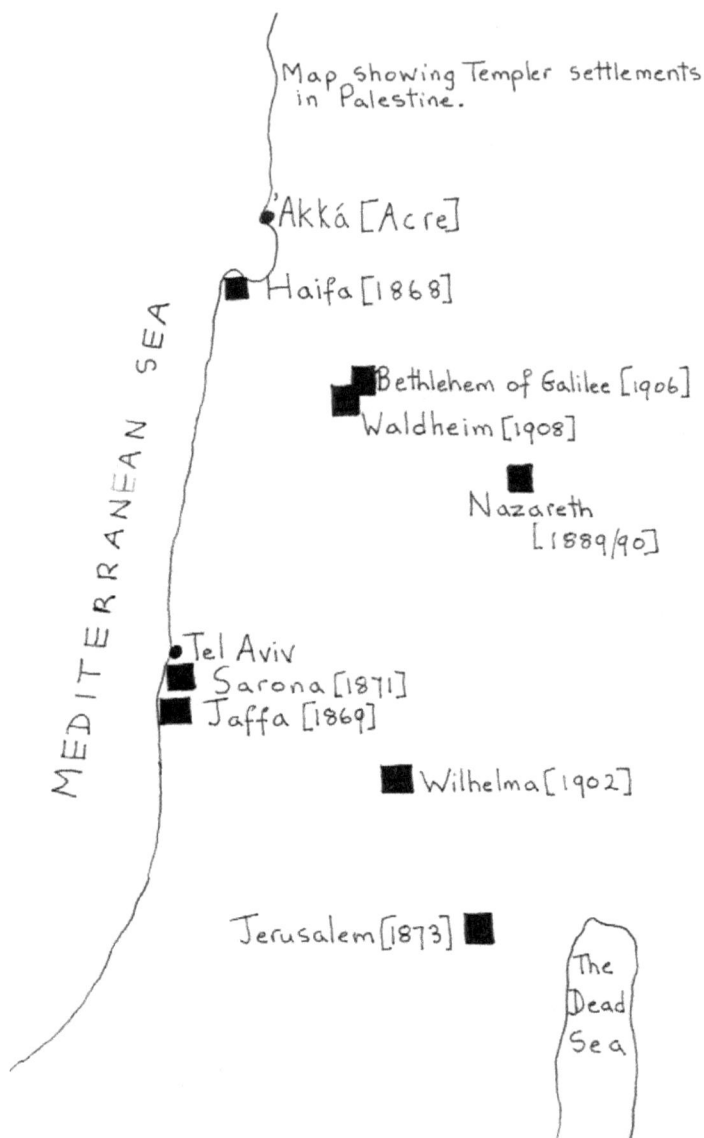

Map showing Templer settlements in Palestine.

'Akká [Acre]

Haifa [1868]

Bethlehem of Galilee [1906]
Waldheim [1908]

Nazareth [1889/90]

MEDITERRANEAN SEA

Tel Aviv
Sarona [1871]
Jaffa [1869]

Wilhelma [1902]

Jerusalem [1873]

The Dead Sea

communities living and working in southern Russia, and the following year Hoffmann, now in his late 60s, left Palestine for the last time, travelling via Stuttgart, in Germany, across the Atlantic to America, where there were several strong and active Templer communities. Hoffmann was accompanied on this tour by his son Samuel, and by Jakob Schumacher, who was still spiritual leader of the Templer settlement in Haifa as well as being the American Consul. Conferences and lectures were given in Buffalo and Schenectady, and the party also visited Templer communities in New York, Baltimore and Philadelphia. It would appear that this rigorous tour took its toll on Hoffmann's health, for shortly after his return from America it became clear that he was suffering both physical and mental decline. At a Temple Festival held in Jerusalem in April 1884 which was attended by Templer representatives from both Russia and Germany, Hoffmann finally resigned as President of the Society, his position being replaced by a Central Committee with Christoph Paulus appointed as chairman. Hoffmann died in Jerusalem in 1885, followed by his wife, Pauline in 1893, a year after Walhalla, a further Templer settlement, was being established just to the north of Jaffa.

The German Consul in Jerusalem believed that with Hoffmann's death, and with continuing disunity in the Templer community, the Society would lose momentum and that many of its followers would return to the Protestant Church. In his opinion their social relationship would survive due to their mutual involvement in industry and trade, but his negative predictions concerning their religious bond neglected to take into consideration the strong spiritual ties which the settlers retained and which ensured a continuation of their religious conviction and activities.

All in all the Templer communities made a success of their economic ventures, and by the beginning of 1889 they were in possession of 166 houses, 67 of which were in Haifa, which also had 63 commercial buildings and a large number of livestock, including cattle, horses, sheep, pigs and goats.[1] Businesses of all types thrived wherever the Templers had established their communities, and included a cheese factory, a soap factory, a brick works, 10 steam-powered mills, one of which was a saw mill, 11 restaurants, an oil press, and two catgut string factories! The 20 or so years leading up to the First World War were relatively successful and lucrative, of particular note being an enterprise in the new settlement at Walhalla, where the Wagner Brothers established what became the largest industrial venture in Palestine, employing 130 staff by 1912. They were noted for their fine design and manufacturing, and amongst their various operations they supplied mills, pumps and engines required for irrigating the orange groves. Other ventures during this period were also proving to be extremely successful; building enterprises contributed to the construction of roads and key buildings, and the hotel trade had taken off in most major towns and cities, including Tiberias, where at the time there were no other hotels worthy of boasting a European standard.

Although most of the Templers who settled in Palestine were eventually successful in their venture, they were nevertheless strongly patriotic, holding on to their German citizenship and maintaining their South German dialect. Therefore, when they heard that the German Kaiser, Wilhelm II, was due to visit Jerusalem in the autumn of 1898 in order to take part in the consecration of the Church of the Redeemer in Jerusalem, they were overjoyed. Due to the dangerous autumn storms to which Jaffa was often subjected, the decision was made for the royal party to disembark at Haifa, which at that time had no appropriate landing stage. This situation was soon rectified when Sultan Abdu'l-Hamid II, who happened to be a friend of the Kaiser, arranged for a new landing to be built, which was designed by a Templer architect and built by a Templer building firm, and which was an extension of the main Templer street running from the foot of Mount Carmel down to the sea.[2]

A fine reception was organized for the Kaiser's arrival in Haifa, and having met with the Templers there and congratulated them on their beautiful German settlement, he moved on to Sarona and Jerusalem, his visit not only helping to advertise the successful Templer settlements but also resulting in innumerable newspaper articles which praised their economic and cultural successes. Four years later, in 1902, having successfully raised funds following three years of hard-won negotiations, the Templers were able to establish another settlement to the east of Jaffa, naming it Wilhelma in honour of King Wilhelm II of Württemberg, whose support and encouragement had been invaluable; this was followed in 1906 by the establishment of a new colony at Bethlehem in Galilee.

In the meantime, the situation for the Bahá'ís who had been living in Akka in the late 1860s and 1870s had also improved, following two years of continuous imprisonment in the confines of the prison barracks during which Bahá'ís who had walked all the way from Persia in order to visit Bahá'u'lláh were restricted to a view of His window from the third, and furthermost moat. Even in the midst of such hardship and suffering Bahá'u'lláh wrote to some of His followers, 'Fear not. These doors shall be opened. My tent shall be pitched on Mount Carmel, and the utmost joy shall be realized.'³

When the barracks were required for housing soldiers the Bahá'í prisoners were moved to various small houses within the town of Akka itself, where for seven years they lived in extremely cramped conditions, devoid of any access to the sight or feel of vegetation. Only after a long and concerted effort by His son, 'Abdu'l-Bahá, was Bahá'u'lláh able to spend two years in a beautiful house outside the city walls, before moving finally, in 1879, to the Mansion of Bahjí. Although He was still ostensibly a prisoner, respect for Bahá'u'lláh was such that not only did He receive requests to visit from officials and generals – which He seldom granted – but He was also greatly admired by the rulers of Palestine.

During these later years Bahá'u'lláh made three visits to Haifa, the first probably during August 1883 and lasting just a few days, during which He stayed in a house in the Templer colony.[4] On a second visit some time in 1890 He spent a few nights in the Oliphant house, a Templer home which Laurence Oliphant had inhabited just before he passed away in 1890.[5] According to Oliphant's biographer, during a year-long visit to Haifa during 1882–83 he and his first wife, Alice, stayed in the house next to that of Gottlieb Schumacher, whose father, Jacob, was head of the Templer colony. Oliphant's biographer notes that 'while "living the life" the Germans of the Temple Society awaited the Second Coming, which, according to them, was almost due, and until then they made olive oil and soap'.[6]

Bahá'u'lláh's third visit, which was His last, took place over three months during the summer of 1891. Having stayed initially in a Templer house in the German colony[7] He then pitched His tent on some land at the base of Mount Carmel, on Hagefen Street, and adjacent to the Templer house on the lintel of which was inscribed, '*Der Herr ist nahe 1871*' (The Lord is nigh 1871).[8] The Pfander family who lived in the house at the time had a young daughter by the name of Wilhelmine, and many years later she recounted that she remembered seeing Bahá'u'lláh's tent on the land next to her home, and that when He was unwell He accepted an invitation to stay in the house, where He was attended by the Templer doctor.[9]

Had members of the Templer community understood the significance of Bahá'u'lláh's claim as stated in His Tablet to Hardegg 20 years earlier, this moment would no doubt have made an impression, and although at the time it passed without mention there were Templers who did, subsequently, understand Bahá'u'lláh's message. Gerhard Schmelzle, for instance, was a Templer who had been born and brought up in Haifa, and who had emigrated with his parents to Australia, where as an adult he became a Bahá'í; and it was his wife who sought out and interviewed Wilhelmine Pfander, who as an adult had also moved from Haifa to Australia.

It was one day during His final stay in Haifa, in 1891, that Bahá'u'lláh, with his son 'Abdu'l-Bahá, walked up the lower slopes of Mount Carmel to where a small circle of about 15 young cypress trees had been planted by Templer Wilhelm Deiss a few years earlier. Also present was Husayn Iqbal, who recorded that from the centre of the cypress trees Bahá'u'lláh indicated to 'Abdu'l-Bahá His desire that the area immediately below them was the spot where a mausoleum should be erected in which the remains of the Báb, the Herald of His own man-ifestation, could finally be laid to rest.[10] Since the land was in the ownership of German Templers at the time, and both Bahá'u'lláh and 'Abdu'l-Bahá were still, by all intents and pur-poses, prisoners, this hope seemed to be an impossibility.

However, following years of frustrating negotiations, 'Abdu'l-Bahá finally managed to procure the land designated for the mausoleum in 1896; it took another ten or more years to acquire the land immediately behind it, where the circle of cypress trees were situated, land still belonging at the time to Templer Wilhelm Deiss. According to Wilhelm's daughter Maria, 'Abdu'l-Bahá visited her father almost every day, occa-sionally asking if he was interested in selling his land, to which Wilhelm's response was always no. It was only when he lost all his produce due to an infection in the vineyard that he decided to sell his land to 'Abdu'l-Bahá, at the same time agreeing to become his gardener. Since Bahá'u'lláh passed away in 1892, He never saw the Báb's resting-place for Himself; He died at Bahjí, His home just outside Akka, where His remains were laid to rest and where Bahá'í pilgrims from all over the world now pay homage.

Before His passing, Bahá'u'lláh had indicated in His will that His son 'Abdu'l-Bahá was to be the authorized interpreter of His teachings and Head of the Faith, and in the years which followed, it was 'Abdu'l-Bahá who, in a continuing life of service, furthered His Father's teachings, promoted peace and unity, and established the early beginnings of Bahá'í institutions. 'Abdu'l-Bahá was just 24 years old when, in 1868, with his family and a few of his Father's followers, he had been exiled to the penal colony of Akka, where conditions had been so terrible that it was expected that all the prisoners would perish. Nevertheless, despite the conditions and extreme tests, most of the Bahá'ís survived, and by the end of 1898 Bahá'ís from the west began travelling to Akka in order to visit 'Abdu'l-Bahá.

The appearance of so many westerners, however, was eventually viewed by the authorities with great suspicion, and as a result 'Abdu'l-Bahá's movements were restricted, until, that is, all political prisoners in the Ottoman Empire were released as a result of the Young Turk Revolution in 1908. By this time 'Abdu'l-Bahá had already started to move members of his family from Akka to a house he had built at the foot of Mount Carmel, in Haifa, and having joined them shortly after the revolution he was able not only to engage with the Templers living around him, but also to benefit from their excellent doctors and their skills in the purchasing of land on Mount Carmel.

And so, for a little while, the Templers and the Bahá'ís found themselves living and working side by side at the base of Mount Carmel. Contemporary records tell of the warm relationship which 'Abdu'l-Bahá enjoyed with some members of the Templer colony, in particular the younger children, with whom he often conversed in fairly acceptable German, and to whom he was wont to give coins or sweets which he kept in the pocket of his gown. One of the children was a girl by the name of Cornelia Wortz, who remembered that her grandfather often chatted to 'Abdu'l-Bahá, once asking him for advice on his wheat crop. When Cornelia became a friend of 'Abdu'l-Bahá's daughters, they often met together on the flat roof of a neighbouring Templer house in order to do embroidery; interestingly, the neighbour's son, Gerhard Bubeck, eventually accepted the Bahá'í Faith. When in 1917 the first aeroplane landed in Haifa, it was Cornelia whom 'Abdu'l-Bahá invited to present a bouquet of flowers to the pilots.[11]

In the years 1911 to 1913 'Abdu'l-Bahá, now in his late 60s, made several trips to the west, including North America, Britain, Germany, France, Austria and Hungary, where the Bahá'í Faith was beginning to spread through the efforts of a few dedicated Bahá'ís, some of whom had visited 'Abdu'l-Bahá in Akka as pilgrims several years earlier. The purpose of 'Abdu'l-Bahá's journeys was to encourage and support the fledgling Bahá'í communities burgeoning in the west, and to further promote Bahá'u'lláh's prescription for spiritual and social renewal.

With the coming of the First World War the relatively peaceful situation in Haifa was soon to change, particularly in relation to the Templers, whose allegiance to Germany brought with it profound difficulties for all the Templer communities living in Palestine, and although conditions improved between the wars, the Second World War saw to it that the Templers' dream of permanently settling in Palestine was finally dashed. As for 'Abdu'l-Bahá, following the constant threat during the Great War both from Allied bombardment and the Turkish commander, the post-war British Mandate over Palestine brought a degree of security and a steady stream of Bahá'í pilgrims. In December 1919, as a result of the humanitarian service he had offered to the British Government in order to protect the population in Palestine from famine during the war, 'Abdu'l-Bahá was awarded a KBE,[12] but although he accepted the title, he never permitted anyone to address him as 'Sir'.

As the Templers in Haifa faced an uncertain future, the Bahá'ís slowly established what would eventually become the Bahá'í World Centre as it is today. A beautiful golden dome now stands over the original mausoleum, and a vast area of Mount Carmel is blessed with magnificent, verdant gardens of surpassing beauty, with nineteen terraces leading from the foot of the mountain where the Templer houses still stand, right to the very summit. To the south of the Shrine of the Báb is an arc of impressive buildings which constitute the administrative buildings of the Bahá'í Faith, envisaged by Bahá'u'lláh in the Tablet of Carmel, which He wrote during His three-month sojourn to Haifa in 1891, stating that God would 'sail His Ark' on Mount Carmel, and that the mountain would be 'the seat of His throne'.[13]

This prediction, at a time when most of the mountain appeared to be an impenetrable mass of rocks, stones, and wild unmanageable scrub, seemed an impossible dream, a hopeless longing; but this was a dream which, with years of planning and hard work, eventually became a reality, transforming Mount Carmel into a beautiful hanging garden rising upwards from the street where the Templers first began building their houses as they strived to fulfil their dreams and their passionate longing to prepare for the coming of God's promised Kingdom on earth.

But destiny had other plans for the Templer community living in Haifa, and by the year 1948 they had left behind their beautiful settlement for ever.

Epilogue

Due to the Templers' allegiance to Germany the First World War brought with it severe hardship for the Templer communities living in Palestine, resulting in a period of intense uncertainty and suffering, only a fraction of which is described here. More than a few Templer men who were of an age for military service received call-up papers, and were joined by volunteers wishing to support their fatherland, many of them losing their lives in battle on the Eastern and Western fronts. From 1915 Walhalla was used as an observation post overlooking the Mediterranean, and at times of extreme danger women and children with homes close to the beach sought safety amongst the sand dunes.

When British forces broke through the Turkish southern front in December 1916 they began building a railway from Egypt, extending it all the way along the Palestine coast as they advanced north, thus enabling the movement of troops and civilians as the war progressed. In February 1917 shelling from the French ship *Jeanne d'Arc* damaged several Templer buildings, including their iron factory which was involved in Turkish military supplies. In the autumn of that year all men of military age (18–48) living in the Southern Templer settlements were moved north to avoid capture by the British troops as they advanced, and by the end of the year any Germans who weren't ill or infirm and who still remained in Jaffa were ordered to evacuate by the British (who accused them of espionage), their final destination the Sidi Bishr internment camp near Alexandria, in Egypt.

The settlement at Wilhelma suffered severe bombardment with resulting damage and casualties during December of that year, and all those who remained following the removal of the men to Alexandria were evacuated to Jaffa. Haifa had been bombed in November 1917 with little damage, falling to the British the following September, and by the end of the year the British had deported women, children, and remaining elderly men still living in the southern Templer settlements by train to an internment camp named Helouan, near Cairo, in Egypt.

Although the Templer internees managed to organize themselves into a functioning community, along with fellow prisoners from both the Roman Catholic and Evangelical Churches, their hope was that the situation wouldn't drag on for too long. However, it was not to be, for two years later they were still there, despite desperate efforts by various official bodies to facilitate their return to their homes in Palestine. By February 1920 the British, keen to close Helouan camp but reluctant to allow the German internees to return to Palestine, were of the mistaken opinion that they would be happy to go back to Germany, despite the fact that most of them, being second or third generation Templers, had been born in Palestine. When the decision to invite volunteers to travel to Germany proved to be unsuccessful, the order was given for 270 to be transported almost immediately, with the remainder following on later.

The voyage from Alexandria was long and rough, severe seasickness and an outbreak of measles amongst the children making it hard to bear. On docking at Hamburg, most of the Templers were taken south to Bad Mergentheim, in Württemberg, where they were given accommodation in a castle which had previously been used as barracks. Plans to transport the remaining 400 Templers back to Germany who still remained in Helouan camp never materialized, and they were transferred, instead, to a former hospital north of Cairo.

The plight of the Templers prevented by Britain from returning to their homes in Palestine became a political talking point in various quarters, including Jewish representatives, the Red Cross, the Quakers, and Protestant communities in England and America. It's hard to imagine the extreme stress that this desperate situation no doubt caused amongst the Templer community.

From early May until late October 1920 the subject of the German Templers was discussed by the British Government in both the House of Commons and the House of Lords. However, despite the fact that Unitarians Lord Newton and Lord Lamington expressed their concern in the House of Lords, the Government was non-committal. In mid-June the Templers who were confined in Bad Mergentheim sent a telegram to the German Government expressing frustration not only with their own internment, but also with that of their family members in Egypt. Again, Lord Newton brought the subject up in the House of Lords, this time receiving a response from Earl Curzon, which despite some initial confusion, did eventually produce positive results. But the process took time and organization, not the least being preparation of Templer property, some of which had been used for other purposes during the war, and although the internees from Egypt arrived home in Palestine at the beginning of September, it wasn't until January 1921 that the settlers from Germany finally landed at Jaffa, where they were greeted with an official welcome from the local musical society.

As far as the purpose of the Templer Society was concerned at this time, its main focus was still the attainment of God's kingdom on earth as Jesus had prophesied, some of those from the older generation expressing their concern that in recent times too much attention had been given to educating the intellect and commercial undertakings, rather than spiritual. However, during a meeting in 1927 it was suggested that bringing God's people together in Jerusalem should no longer be the main focus of their work, a sentiment which greatly disappointed many Templers.

During the 1920s most of the Templer communities enjoyed a degree of economic stability, Haifa, for instance, with its railway and busy port, fast becoming a hub of economic development in Palestine; indeed, the settlement there enjoyed a wide range of cultural opportunities, including a music society, two choirs, a literary society, a sports club, and a young mens' association. However, the German homeland was far from forgotten, and if anything, attachment to it had strengthened following the war, the Central Council in Jerusalem maintaining close contact with the Regional Council in Stuttgart, where the *Sentinel* was still being published.

Towards the end of the First World War, on 2 November 1917, the British Foreign Minister, Lord Balfour, had issued a statement regarding the future of Palestine. Known as the Balfour Declaration, it stated that the British Government was in favour of establishing in Palestine a national home for the Jewish people. A few years later the *Sentinel* began publishing material related to the Jewish–Arab question regarding ownership rights, and for the most part the Templers endeavoured to live in harmony with their Jewish neighbours as the latter expanded their various industrial and agricultural initiatives. Indeed, although following their return to Palestine the *Sentinel* had expressed some criticism of Zionism, a visitor was able to report in 1927 that there was no evidence at all of anti-Semitic feeling amongst the Templers.

On 30 January 1933, Adolph Hitler was appointed German Chancellor. For the Germans living in Palestine this was simply a matter of one government being succeeded by another, and they certainly had no notion of the serious situation which was about to unfold. But their attitude was soon severely criticized by the State Party Group Leader for Palestine, a certain Cornelius Schwartz, who often enjoyed an active role in the Templer Society, and who, believing that the leaders of the Temple Society were opposed to the National Socialist movement, accused them of lacking moral fibre.[1]

When the German Consulates of Jerusalem and Jaffa were instructed to fly the Reich flag (black, white and red) and the swastica, a number of Templers supported the Zionist community in requesting the Consulates to remove them, which the Consulates felt unable to do. This was just the beginning of the trials to come, trials which within a very short space of time would change the lives of the German Templers forever, for already some of the younger generation were beginning to favour the new German Reich. No one at that time could have foreseen the horrendous events to come.

In April 1933 moves were made which resulted in the boycotting of Jewish businesses, and as a result of this and the rise of the Hitler regime in Germany, Jewish suspicion of the German communities living amongst them in Palestine mounted. A month later Hitler's belief in the creation of a national community was quoted in the *Sentinel*, greatly inspiring many of the Templer readers; under its editor, Templer Dietrich Lange, who believed that National Socialist ideology wasn't dissimilar to that of the Templers, the *Sentinel* gradually became a vehicle for publishing Nazi propaganda rather than religious subjects, and in late 1935 it printed Hitler's closing speech at the Nuremberg Reich Party Conference, during which new laws were proclaimed, including the exclusion of Jews from the German community and virtually labelling them as second-class citizens. This suited Dietrich Lange, who not only embraced anti-Semitism, but also announced publicly that he had abandoned the Old Testament as being a 'load of old rubbish from the religious junk room'.[2]

When the President (Christian Rohrer) of the Temple Society died as a result if an accident in May 1934, so too did certain strong beliefs and opinions which had held the community together since the First World War. So far as Rohrer was concerned, Hitler's book *Mein Kampf* was trivial, and he certainly didn't believe that as a religious body the Temple Society should associate its members with a political party. Following his death and a Temple Council meeting early in 1935, the new Constitution confirmed that their long-term task was still the establishment of God's Kingdom on earth, although emphasis on the Bible in shaping their spiritual belief was no longer fundamental to their Christian journey. The new President, (Philipp Wurst) was also Mayor of the Haifa Templer settlement, and he keenly stressed the importance of regarding Christ as their spiritual leader, thus clearly indicating that there should be a clear distinction between the Society and Nazi ideology, a view which, needless to say, didn't go down too well with the National Socialist German Workers Party (NSDAP), or the National Socialist Party. But despite his reservations, Wurst nevertheless admitted that some aspects of National Socialism did interest him, even claiming during a lecture in Jaffa that certain beliefs expressed in a book, *The Myth of the Twentieth Century*, by Nazi writer Alfred Rosenberg were in accord with the Templer's religious views.

As National Socialism took control in Germany, Nazi groups also became established in Palestine; every German settlement had its own NSDAP association where Hitler Youth groups offered a full diary of events, the younger generation feeling inspired by what the party stood for. And as enthusiasm for the new regime grew, so did anti-Semitism, which in the early days of political training was high on the agenda. Trips to the fatherland were organized in order to encourage the young people in their allegiance to the Party, propaganda films were shown in the German cinema in Jerusalem, and in Serona the Chairman of the Templer Community not only announced his loyalty to National Socialism, but also expressed his firm conviction that the objectives of the movement were in harmony with the Templer Society's hope of creating God's kingdom. The Templer settlements at Waldheim and Bethlehem were particularly active in National Socialist work, and reports sent to the fatherland noted that, generally speaking, communities living in towns were less receptive than those in the country, voicing criticism of certain Templer leaders who were complaining of NSDAP intrusion into their religious concerns. But the Templers themselves weren't unanimous in their views, and it was

the hope of the NSDAP that those who were as yet uncon-
vinced would soon join those who already recognized in the
National Socialist movement a realization of their own goals.
In December 1935 the 50th anniversary of Hoffmann's
death was commemorated by the placing of a wreath on his
grave by an NSDAP official, in acknowledgment of the success of the Templer Society communities; a further message
not only congratulated Hoffmann on his dedication to his
homeland and all it stood for, but also expressed the hope that
the Society would collaborate with the local NSDAP organization in a shared vision of national community. Although these
sentiments were a far cry from the early beginnings of the Templer Society with its pure intentions focused on the Bible and
Christ's promises, it's as well to remember, firstly, that it is only
with hindsight that we can wonder at how such an ideal vision
could so quickly lose its original goals, and secondly, that not
all Templers travelled the National Socialist road. Indeed,
efforts were made to counter the influence of the NSDAP, and
music societies within the Templer settlements made a concerted effort to encourage musical performance and audience
participation, probably as a way of appealing to the higher
spiritual nature and combatting political susceptibilities.

In the meantime the *Sentinel* continued to publish material
praising Hitler, even suggesting in February 1937 that he had
offered the Germans a constructive religious model replacing
the disaster which Bolshevism would inevitably have brought
had it succeeded. Regular reports continued to appear in the
Sentinel over the following year, focused on Hitler's various
speeches as well as mounting support for National Socialism
and its shared ideals with the Temple Society. However, there
was no mention at all of the *Kristallnacht* (Crystal Night) on
9/10 November 1938, which proved to be a defining moment
in the build-up to the start of the Second World War a year
later.[3]

The Second World War began on 1 September 1939, when

German troops invaded Poland, the Templer settlement in Haifa already feeling its effect a day later when it found itself surrounded by British and Jewish police. Germans were ordered to stay off the streets, shops were closed, and on 3 September all men of military age who hadn't already left the country in order to escape capture by the British were sent to an internment camp at Akka, later being transferred to Jaffa. The farming settlements of Sarona, Wilhelma, Bethlehem in Galilee and Waldheim were turned into large internment camps by the British Mandate government, each of them surrounded by barbed wire and watchtowers and guarded by Arab and Jewish police serving under British command. For the time being women and children from the German colonies in Jerusalem, Jaffa and Haifa were able to stay in their own homes, albeit under surveillance of Jewish and British police. Once every month the internees were lined up in order to be inspected by a CIA official, with the leader of the Temple Society, Nikolai Schmidt, later complaining that the enormous file of evidence concerning the Templers' hostile behaviour was pure fiction, and insisting that they were a trustworthy and decent community.

In July 1941 the British Mandatory Authorities decided to move most able-bodied Germans and their families who were still living in Palestine well away from the front line, and despite protests from the German Government they nevertheless went ahead, deporting 665 men, women and children as far away as possible; of these, 536 were Templers, the rest being members of the Evangelical and Roman Catholic denominations. The Templers left their homes with a bare minimum of possessions, those in the north beginning the journey on a train from Haifa and joining those from the south at Lydd, north west of Jerusalem. The long tortuous journey by train and ferry eventually took them to an ocean liner waiting for them in the Red Sea, and still, as they set sail towards the Gulf of Aden, they had no idea what their final destination might be.

They had been at sea for some time when it slowly dawned on them that they were, in fact, on their way to Australia, finally sailing into Sydney Harbour on 23 August; the journey then continued overland by train, which arrived 24 hours later at the Tatura internment camp at Rushworth, 176 kilometres north of Melbourne. With the benefit of hindsight it's difficult to comprehend how it was that various National Socialist activities, including those involving Nazi Youth and the League of German Girls, were allowed to continue when the German Templers arrived in Australia; indeed, efforts were made by the Camp Command at Tatura to ban them, although the Hitler salute wasn't prohibited until April 1944, nearly three years after their arrival at the camp. Once again, it's worth remembering that not all members of the Templer Society were Nazi sympathizers.

As the Templers in Australia slowly adapted to camp life as internees, those left at home in Palestine also faced enormous challenges. According to Cornelius Schwartz, who was still State Group Leader in Palestine, 1,052 German internees, including Templers and members of other Christian denominations, were still in Palestine, although with the deportation of so many to Australia, agricultural productivity wasn't as easy to manage as it had been before the hostilities. The settlements at Sarona and Wilhelma, for instance, were surrounded by barbed wire fences and guarded from watchtowers by Jewish guards who were under British command, but despite these restrictions the internal affairs of the camps were allowed to function normally, with organized visits between the various camps made possible at Christmas and Easter.

However, this manageable existence soon deteriorated when, following Germany's unconditional surrender on 8 May 1945, the magnitude of the horrific atrocities against the Jews by the Nazi regime were revealed. The Templers, in particular, were targeted, even though not all of them had been affiliated with the Nazi movement, and indeed, many of the allegations made against them were unfounded. They were keen to stress that as Germans living outside their homeland they had felt honour bound to recognize the government in power and to obey its laws regardless of whether they agreed with them or not, and later commenting that although many Templers had believed in the Hitler regime, they challenged anyone to find a Jew in Palestine who had suffered at their hands, alluding to the successful development of Palestine largely due to their hard work and perseverance.

Despite the difficulties the Templers faced after the war in Palestine, they were keen to remain there, and when the Mandatory Government informed them that the intention was to return them to Germany, the leaders of both the Templer Society and the Lutheran community pointed out that their reason for settling in Palestine had been religious, that the majority of them had been born there, and that by being forced into returning to Germany they would not only lose their homes but also become impoverished refugees.

In the meantime, by the end of 1946 life had improved considerably for the Templers who had been deported to Australia, for they had been allowed to leave the camps and were in the process of settling permanently. They were distressed by the situation which their fellow believers in Palestine were facing, and so it was with this in mind that they approached the immigration minister with a view to allowing them to emigrate to Australia. There followed nearly two years of uncertainty as the situation was discussed and mulled over by the various parties involved, until in April 1948 circumstances brought it to a head, when the Waldheim settlement was attacked in an armed raid by 'Soldiers of the Jewish Secret Army' (Haganah) who, having killed an old Templer couple, locked the rest of the residents in the dairy, where the Jewish army leader proceeded to remind them of their terrible crimes against the Jews. As far as the British were concerned this vicious attack was the catalyst for evacuating as many Templers as possible from the perimeter settlements with immediate effect, those too infirm or old to travel being transferred to the settlement in Jerusalem, which remained intact. Freed by a British military unit and given 20 minutes to collect belongings from their wrecked homes, the Germans were taken to a military camp in Akka before boarding a troop ship at Haifa. On 21 April 1948, with bullets firing over the ship, the Templers sailed out of the bay of Haifa.[4]

The first leg of the journey took the Germans to Cyprus, where on 22 April they were installed temporarily in the Golden Sands holiday camp on the beach. However, it soon became clear that the term 'temporary' was open-ended, and it wasn't until mid-October that 49 settlers who had chosen to return to Germany were flown home. The first group bound for Australia sailed in mid-December, their excitement greatly enhanced by the discovery of a stowaway in a packing case, apparently a former prisoner of war who had formed a liaison with one of the young settlers. This group of 37 Germans landed in Sydney on 11 January 1949, and on 26th 45 further camp inmates flew out of Nicosia, with 170 sailing from Famagusta. The 77 remaining at the Golden Sands holiday camp didn't depart until 9 March, reaching Melbourne on 3 April.

Although the leader of the Templer Society, Nikolai Schmidt, had been hopeful of retaining the Templer settlement at Rephaim, Jerusalem, this unfortunately didn't materialize, and following several life-threatening attacks during the early part of 1948 the remaining Templers sought refuge in a Catholic hospice under the authority of the Red Cross, the Sisters of the Order of St. Borromaeus. Conditions were cramped, and religious services were curtailed in the strict Catholic domain, and so when in March 1949 the Templers were allowed to return to their empty homes they were relieved to be able to resume at least some of their former activities. It was during this period that Christoph Hoffmann's grandson, Dr. Wilhelm Hoffmann, died after a long illness.

Nikolai Schmidt's dream of remaining in Jerusalem soon proved to be too difficult to sustain, particularly in regard to work, which became hard to come by for non-Jewish citizens, and on 14 November 1949 several Templer families were asked to leave, membership of the NSDAP being given as the prime reason. Protesting against this demand was deemed pointless, and although many more families joined the expulsion list, the authorities were so slow in administering the order that it wasn't until the end of the year that the exodus began, a few choosing Germany but most opting for Australia. Just eleven fragile and elderly Templers remained in Jerusalem, to be cared for at the Catholic hospice. Nikolai Schmidt lamented this sad moment in the history of the German Templers, as did, no doubt, many devoted Templers at that time, as they looked back to the early days of their extraordinary settlement project in Palestine, which had begun with such faith and optimism 80 years previously, and which was now no more than a remnant of Christoph Hoffmann's dream.

Despite such enormous challenges, however, the Temple Society lived on, and continues to live on, both in Germany and in Australia, where by 1950 it was developing centres in Melbourne, Sydney and Adelaide, its official name now the Temple Society Australia with Dr Richard O. Hoffmann, a great-grandson of Christoph Hoffmann, as Regional Head. In 1962 the Society was finally reimbursed by Israel for the loss of its properties in Palestine, (approximately £65 million by current values) and in 1970 the Australian and German Templers were formally linked by the appointment of Dr. Richard O. Hoffmann as President of the Temple Society. By 2005 the Society considered itself as consisting of many interest and focus groups rather than a community-based organization, and changed its constitution accordingly. The Temple Society is active to this day both in Australia and in Germany, where it is centred on the community facility in the Degerloch district of Stuttgart.

Appendix

Lawḥ-i Hartik

The Tablet of Bahá'u'lláh to Georg David Hardegg

Translation and commentary by Stephen N. Lambden,* with additional notes by Jeremy Fox

(The paragraphs are numbered for convenience.)

1

In the name of God, the Most Holy.
Thy sealed letter arrived before the Wronged One. Therefrom did We catch a fragrance of thy sincerity towards God, the Protector, the Self Subsisting. We entreat God that He might inform thee of that which is concealed in an inscribed Tablet; might enable thee to hearken unto the cooing of the Dove upon the branches and the murmuring of the Water of Life which hath flowed with Wisdom and Explanation from the spring of the Will of the King of Existence.

2

O beloved one!
It is necessary that thine eminence contemplate the Word of God, the grandeur and sweetness of which sufficeth all the worlds. The first of those who believed in the Spirit [Jesus] was enraptured by the Word of his Lord and through it turned and believed, detached from whatsoever the people possess. Such action is incumbent upon the fishes of the Most Great Ocean.

---

* This provisional translation was originally published in *Bahá'í Studies Bulletin*, vol. 2, no. 1 (June 1983). Revised 2004–2015.

3

O Thou informed mystic knower and insightful religious leader!

Know thou that base passion hath hindered most mortals from turning their faces unto God, the King of Names. Such, however, as gaze with the eye of insight, shall bear witness and seeing, exclaim, 'Praise be unto my Lord, the Most Exalted.' Land and sea hath rejoiced at the Beneficence of God. The nations were given the promise regarding the appearance of the Healer of Infirmities. He, assuredly, is the expected Builder of the Temple. Blessed be such as are possessed of mystic knowledge. When the appointed time came, Carmel cried out, trembling as if shaken by the breezes of the Lord, 'Blessed be such as hearken!' Should anyone incline with the ear of the inner nature, the same would assuredly hear the cry from the Rock. It, verily, proclaimeth in a most elevated voice and beareth witness unto the Eternal God. Blessed be such as catch a fragrance of the Utterance and turn unto the Kingdom, detached from the contingent world. When that which is mentioned in the Holy Books hath come to pass, thou shalt see the people beholding but not understanding.

4

O beloved one!

Behold the mystery of reversal on account of the symbol of the Ruler for He hath made their exalted ones their lowly ones and their lowly ones their exalted ones. And call thou to mind the fact that when Jesus came He was rejected by the divines, the learned and the educated. He who was a mere fisherman [Peter], on the other hand, entered the Kingdom. This is the mystery of what was mentioned in the heart of the words by means of intimations and allusions.

5

Great, great is the Cause of God!
Peter the Apostle, in spite of his excellence and the eminence of
his station, held back his tongue when asked about it. Shouldst
thou consider sincerely what hath heretofore come to pass, for
the sake of the Lord alone, thou wilt assuredly see the Light
shining before thine eyes. The Truth is too manifest to be
wrapped up in veils, the Path too open to be enveloped in darkness and the Certainty too evident to be obscured by doubts.
Those who have been held back are the ones who have followed
their lusts and are today slumbering, sleeping. They shall wake
up and run around but find no place to hide. Blessed be such
as catch the fragrance of Truth, then awaken, that they might
attain whatsoever the sincere servants attained.

6

Know thou that We saw the exterior letter Ṣād (ص) in the word
'Peace' (ṣulḥ) (Ar. صُلْح ṣulḥ). It, verily, was adorned with the
ornament of the upright letter Alif, 'A' (= ا) and is what hath
assuredly been mentioned in an Outspread Tablet. And upon
the manifestation of the lights of that Divine Word, the Gate
of Heaven was opened and the Kingdom of Names appeared.
And this matter was completed through the letter 'H' (ه) after
which it was united to the levelled letter 'A' (alif = —) which was
adorned with the Point (• of the letter 'B' = ب) from which the
Treasured Name, the Hidden Mystery and the Guarded Symbol
(بهاء = Bahá) emerged. It, verily, is the Point (•) from which
existence hath appeared and unto which it hath returned.

7

Then We saw the Word which uttered a Word which every
community found to be according to its own tongue and

language. When that Word was uttered, a Sun shone forth from the Horizon of its Announcement, the Lights of which eclipsed the sun of the heavens. It said, 'The head of the seventy hath been adorned with the crown of the forty and been united with the seven before the ten.' Then it lamented and it said, 'What is this that I see? The house doth not recognise its master neither doth the son pay heed unto his father; nor likewise is the hopeful seeker cognisant of his place of refuge and haven.'

8

O thou who soarest in the atmosphere of mystic knowledge! Whoso knoweth the One in Whose Person what floweth yet exhibiteth solidity; what soareth yet is at rest; what is manifest yet concealed and what is resplendent yet veiled, shall be seized by the attraction of the divine Effulgences to such an extent that he will fly on the wings of yearning in the atmosphere of nearness, holiness and reunion.

9

With regard to that which thine eminence hath mentioned concerning the darkness, We bear witness that it hath encompassed the creatures. Blessed be he who hath been illumined by the Light which shineth forth from the horizon of the Mercy of his Lord, the Most Holy. The darkness is the vain imaginings by virtue of which the people were prevented from turning towards the Kingdom when the King of the Divine Realm appeared with the Cause of God.

10

As for what thou hast mentioned, that a certain person hath supposed that there are no differences between us with regard to the Spirit [Jesus], this is indeed the truth inasmuch as the

Spirit [Jesus] is sanctified beyond being overwhelmed by differences or encompassed by symbolic expressions. He, verily, is the Light of Oneness among mankind and the sign of the Ancient of Days among the peoples. He who turneth unto Him [Jesus] hath turned unto He [God] who sent Him [Jesus] and he who rejecteth Him hath rejected He who caused Him to be made manifest and to speak forth. He hath ever been what He was and will ever remain the same as what He was; only the Effulgence of His Theophany in the Mirrors varies on account of Their different forms and colours.

11

O beloved one!

Should a hint of the secret which was veiled in mystery be disclosed, the hearts of those who cling unto what they possess and cast away what is with God would be thrown into confusion. If thine eminence would ponder upon what We have set forth for thee and rise up according to what hath been mentioned with the greatest steadfastness, there would, verily, be manifest from thee what was previously made manifest.

12

O beloved one!

This Bird is ensnared betwixt the talons of oppression and hypocrisy, and seest no nest wherein he might dwell nor any retreat unto which he might wing his way. In such a state doth He summon mankind unto everlasting life. Blessed be the attentive ear! We ask God that he might bring us together in the same place and might assist us in what He loveth and is well pleasing unto Him.

Two short commentaries on the Tablet of Baha'u'llah to Georg David Hardegg

Commentary by Stephen N. Lambden (written for this book at the author's request)

The Lawḥ-i Hartik ('Tablet for Hardegg') is a two or three page Arabic scriptural Tablet (lawḥ), letter, or epistle of Mirza Husayn 'Ali Nuri (1817–1892), entitled Baha'u'llah (The Glory of God), the founder of the Baha'i religion. Most likely written between late 1871 and mid-1872, its basic purpose was to inform the Templer co-founder and leader, Georg David Hardegg (and others), that biblical and related Islamic prophecies pertaining to the latter days or the expected 'end-time', had come to pass or were finding an ongoing contemporary realization. Hardegg had tried to meet Baha'u'llah but was only able to meet his son 'Abdu'l-Baha (d. 1921), although he subsequently became the recipient of this weighty communication. As the new 'Temple' is centred in the Divine persona of Baha'u'llah the eschatological Paraclete ('Comforter', see below), it is he who should be sought rather than a renewed, concrete third Temple located in Jerusalem or elsewhere.

At the commencement of this text, Hardegg is addressed as a person of deep visionary learning, as one 'beloved' and an 'informed mystic knower and insightful religious leader'. He is counselled to consider the biblical 'Word of God' that engenders faith. Base thoughts should be transcended such that it might be realized that Baha'u'llah is the promised 'Healer of Infirmities' and the expected messianic 'Builder of the Temple' (see Zechariah 6:12–13). Mount Carmel near Haifa (not Jerusalem), in the state of trembling rapture, is pictured uttering a beatitude upon such as are receptive to the Baha'i message. Such as are possessed of inward 'hearing' might hear a cry of proclamation from that 'Rock' which perhaps represents the Jerusalem Temple, the Jerusalem 'Dome of the Rock'. In this light another beatitude is pronounced upon those who 'catch a fragrance' of the 'Utterance' of eschatological fulfilment and proclamation.

Reference is then made to the cryptic Islamic phrase, 'the mystery of reversal (sir al-tankis) on account of the symbol of the Ruler (ramz al-ra'is)'. This mysterious prophecy is interpreted in terms of the fulfilment of the Islamo–Biblical expectation of an impending reversal of faith status, when those 'first' in piety or prestige become the unbelieving 'last' in faith status. Simon Peter, for example, was once a lowly fisherman but ascended, through his faith in Jesus and his word, to a position of pre-eminence.

The spiritual initiation of a long-awaited period of millennial 'Peace' (sulh) is alluded to by means of the first Arabic letter (the letter ص or ṣād) in the Arabic word 'Peace'. This in connection with the advent of Baha'u'llah, the quintessence of whose title or Name, is the word Baha' (Arabic = b + h+ a+'), indicating radiant divine 'glory' or 'splendour', which is related to the second advent of Christ in the 'glory' of the Father or with 'glory' (Greek doxa). From the locus of this 'Treasured Name', 'Hidden Mystery' and 'Guarded Symbol', which is the 'Greatest Name of God', existence had its generative origin and is associated with its eschatological 'return'.

Baha'u'llah refers in the middle of the Lawh-i Hartik to the 'Word which uttered a Word'. This is probably an allusion to Jesus making reference to the mystery of his second coming and the universal message of the future messianic 'Comforter'" the Arabic spelling of which (al-mu`azzi) is spelled out in alphabetical, numerological terms (see John Chapters 14–16). He would address all humanity according to their own language, like the global outreach of the Holy Spirit at Pentecost (see Acts of the Apostles Chapter 2).

The reference through a fourfold divine syzygy type series of 'opposites' (flowing–solid; soaring–resting; manifest–concealed; resplendent–veiled), may point to the universal,

All-Encompassing 'Temple' of the person of Baha'u'llah, who came unknown like a 'thief in the night', generally unrecognized by Christians and others, yet on another level is of transcendent holiness. For Baha'u'llah, eschatological 'darkness', as Hardegg himself had made reference to in an earlier communication, indicates human 'vain imaginings' which inhibit spiritual attainment.

It is the case that there are little or 'no differences between' Christians or Templer Christians and Baha'is in their Christology, their salvific theology regarding Jesus 'the Spirit'. This Baha'u'llah states since the founder of Christianity is 'sanctified beyond being overwhelmed by differences or encompassed by symbolic expressions'. Jesus is the 'Light of Oneness among mankind' and a sign of Baha'u'llah, the 'Ancient of Days'. No change has ever existed or might ever be found in the sanctified being of Jesus Christ.

Towards the conclusion of his Lawh-i Hartik, Baha'u'llah promises Hardegg that should he ponder upon this scriptural Tablet and become one of steadfast faith, he would exhibit and maintain his religious faith. His religio-spiritual status would be maintained. It ends with a lament over the constraints of 'oppression and hypocrisy' which might imply his current imprisonment and the lack of receptivity of his contemporaries. Despite this, Baha'u'llah utters a beatitude upon those receptive, and expresses the hope that God might enable Hardegg to enter his presence and lend assistance in 'what He loveth and is well pleasing unto Him'.

Commentary by Jeremy Fox (written for this book at the author's request)

A brief look at Bahá'u'lláh's circumstances at the time he wrote his letter to George Hardegg is helpful in understanding both its content and its message. At the time the Lawḥ-i-Hartik [Hardegg] was written Bahá'u'lláh was confined in the house of 'Údí Khammár (in late 1871–early 1872?) and did not wish, at a time when the inhabitants of 'Akká viewed him with great suspicion, to draw attention to his lofty claims. His earlier, more explicit 'Tablets to the kings and rulers' were probably not openly or freely circulated in the Haifa–'Akká area at this time. The local Christians living in 'Akká at this time – about 3,000 of them making up one third of 'Akká's inhabitants – were probably not aware that Bahá'-Alláh claimed to be the return of Christ or the promised 'Comforter'. Hardegg had to be content with a veiled declaration by Bahá'u'lláh which he may not have been able to understand.[1]

As indicated, Bahá'u'lláh had already been completely open about his claims in other documents, but not locally, where his circumstances and those of his family and the other Bahá'ís were of a quite perilous nature. Thus, to a certain extent, Hardegg would have had to 'read between the lines' in order to realize the full implications of the message being conveyed.

Having confirmed Hardegg's sincere belief in God Bahá'u'lláh indicates, in poetic language, that he has brought a further revelation (the 'Water of Life') and with it 'Wisdom and Explanation' flowing from a Divine spring. He then asks Hardegg to reflect on the 'Word of God' of which Jesus was the embodiment ('the Word made flesh', John 1:14) and makes reference to Peter as the first to believe in him. Bahá'u'lláh continues by referring, somewhat obliquely, to his own revelation, 'the Most Great Ocean', a term he often used to refer to His Writings; and so the 'fish' are the Bahá'ís. If we jump to paragraph 4 in which Bahá'u'lláh talks about the 'mystery of reversal', he illustrates this concept by pointing out that when Jesus came the learned clergy rejected him, while Peter, a simple fisherman, recognized him and 'entered the Kingdom', so that in God's eyes their ranks were 'reversed'.

In paragraph 3, in which Bahá'u'lláh speaks of the 'Healer

of Infirmities', he appears to be referring to John's vision of the 'new Jerusalem' and how

> in the midst of the street of it, and on either side of the river, [was there] the tree of life, which bare twelve [manner of] fruits, [and] yielded her fruit every month: and the leaves of the tree [were] for the *healing of the nations* (Rev. 22:2).

Bahá'u'lláh links it with the 'expected Builder of the Temple', and seems to be indicating that he is the one who has brought a message 'for the healing of the nations' and that the new Jerusalem and the rebuilding of the Temple are symbolic images, once again the 'Word made flesh' manifested in the human temple of God's chosen one.

As suggested by Lambden in his commentary above, the 'Rock' could be a reference to Jerusalem in which is the Dome of the Rock. Carmel is significant of course for Hardegg in that the Templers' settlement lies at the foot of Mount Carmel with all its biblical associations. Bahá'u'lláh closes this section by saying many will behold these things, yet not understand their significance.

In paragraph 9 Bahá'u'lláh responds to Hardegg's reference to 'darkness' and indicates that he has brought heavenly 'light' and rather more clearly refers to the revelation he has brought: 'The darkness is the vain imaginings by virtue of which the people were prevented from turning towards the Kingdom when the King of the Divine Realm appeared with the Cause of God.'

Bahá'u'lláh then confirms what Hardegg has understood, namely that Bahá'ís believe that by turning to Jesus people are turning to God who sent him and concludes by saying that if Hardegg would 'ponder upon what We have set forth for thee' and act accordingly, he would be manifesting the same perceptivity as Peter, and he finally openly states that he is '[summoning] mankind unto everlasting life'.

Bibliography

Bahá'u'lláh. *Gleanings from the Writings of Bahá'u'lláh.* Trans. Shoghi Effendi. Wilmette, IL: Bahá'í Publishing Trust, 2nd ed. 1976.

— *Tablets of Bahá'u'lláh Revealed after the Kitáb-i-Aqdas.* Comp. Research Department of the Universal House of Justice. Haifa: Bahá'í World Centre, 1978.

Balyuzi, H. M. *Bahá'u'lláh, the King of Glory.* Oxford, George Ronald, 1980.

British North American Wesleyan Methodist Magazine. Vol. 2 (1842). Saint John, NB: Connexional Authority.

Britten, Emma Hardinge. *Nineteenth Century Miracles; or, Spirits and Their Work in Every Country of the Earth: A Complete Historical Compendium of the Great Movement Known as 'Modern Spiritualism'.* Manchester: E. W. Allen, 1884.

Burk, John C. F. *A Memoir of the Life and Writings of John Albert Bengel: Prelate in Würtemberg.* Trans. R. F. Walker. London: William Ball, 1837.

Cunningham, Andrew; Grell, Ole Peter. *The Four Horsemen of the Apocalypse: Religion, War, Famine and Death in Reformation Europe.* Cambridge: Cambridge University Press. 2008.

Day, Michael V. *Journey to a Mountain.* Oxford: George Ronald, 2017.

Duggan, Lawrence G. *Armsbearing and the Clergy in the History and Canon Law of Western Christianity.* Woodbridge, UK and Rochester, NY: Boydell Press, 2013.

Edwards, Mark U. Jr. *Luther's Last Battles: Politics and Polemics.* Minneapolis: Fortress Press, 1985.

Esslemont, J. E. *Bahá'u'lláh and the New Era.* Wilmette IL: Bahá'í Publishing Trust, 1980.

The Christian Observer. Periodical. London: J. Hatchard and Son, 1802–1874.

Fudge, Thomas A. *Jan Hus: Religious Reform and Social Revolution in Bohemia.* London: I. B Tauris, 2010.

Gilly, W. S. *Vigilantius and His Times*: London: Seeley, Burnside and Seeley, 1844.

Global Anabaptist Mennonite Encyclopaedia Online (GAMEO). Available at: gameo.org.

Greenfield, John. *Power from on High: The Story of the Great Moravian Revival of 1727.* London: Marshall, Morgan & Scott, 1928.

Henderson, Philip. *The Life of Laurence Oliphant.* London: Robert Hale, 1956.

Hoffmann, Christoph. *Mein Weg nach Jerusalem* (1884). *Jerusalem Journey: The Autobiography of Christopher Hoffmann, 1815–1885.* Trans. and abridged Gertrud Paulus Reno. Stuttgart: Maria-Paulus-Foundation, 1969.

Howitt, William. 'The Baroness Barbara Juliana von Krüdener', in *The Spiritual Magazine*, vol. IV (1 January 1969), pp. 5–26.

Isaacs, Mark D. 'The end-time calculation of Johann Albrecht Bengel', in *Journal of Unification Studies*, vol. 11, 2010.

Josephus, Flavius. *The Works of Flavius Josephus.* William Whiston. Vol. 1: *Antiquities of the Jews.* London: Thomas Tegg, 1825.

'Krüdener, Barbara Juliana, Baroness von', in *Encyclopedia Britannica* (1911), vol. 15. Available at: https://en.wikisource.org/.

Lambden, Stephen N. 'A Tablet of Bahá'-Alláh to Georg David Hardegg: The Lawḥ-i Hartīk', with additions and revisions November 2004 –2015 (in progress). University of California at Merced: Hurqalya Publications, Center for Shaykhī and Bābī-Bahā'ī Studies. Available at: https://hurqalya.ucmerced.edu/node/237/. The translation was originally published in *Bahá'í Studies Bulletin*, vol. 2, no. 1 (June 1983). Available at: https:/hurqalya.ucmerced.edu/node/239/.

— 'Some notes and commentary on the Lawh-i Hartik, Part Two', University of California at Merced: Hurqalya Publications, Center for Shaykhī and Bābī-Bahā'ī Studies. Available at: https:/hurqalya.ucmerced.edu/ node/240/.

Leake, William Martin. *Journal of a Tour in Asia Minor with Comparative Remarks on the Ancient and Modern Geography of that Country.* London: John Murray, 1824.

Loughborough, J. N. *The Great Second Advent Movement: Its Rise and Progress* (1905). Fort Oglethorpe, GA: Teach Services, 2013.

Luther, Martin. 'Colloquia oder Tischreden', in *D. Martin Luther's Works*, Weimar edition (WA). 6 vols. Available at the Internet Archive, www. archive.org.

Michael, Emily. 'John Wyclif on body and mind', in *Journal of the History of Ideas*, vol, 64 (2003), no. 3.

Momen, Moojan (ed.). *The Bábí and Bahá'í Religions, 1844–1944: Some Contemporary Western Accounts.* Oxford: George Ronald, 1981.

Murray, Thomas. *The Life of John Wycliffe.* Edinburgh: John Boyd, 1829.

New World Encyclopedia. Available at: www. newworldencyclopedia.org.

Oyer, John S. *Lutheran Reformers Against Anabaptists: Luther, Melanchthon and Menius and the Anabaptists of Central Germany.* The Hague: M. Nijhoff, 1964.

Petersen, Rodney L. *Preaching in the Last Days: The Theme of 'Two Witnesses' in the 16th and 17th Centuries.* New York: Oxford University Press, 1993.

Ratliff, Walter R. *Pilgrims on the Silk Road: A Muslim–Christian Encounter in China.* Eugene, OR: WIPF & Stock, 2010.

'Religious character of the late Emperor Alexander', in *The Christian Observer*, vol. XXX, no. 340 (April 1830), pp. 197–207. Available online.

Rogers, Jay. 'Two views of civil government: Puritanism vs. Pietism', in *The Forerunner*, 1 May 2008. Available at: www. forerunner.com.

Rosenberg, Alfred. *Der Mythus des zwanzigsten Jahrhunderts* (1930). *The Myth of the Twentieth Century: An Evaluation of the Spiritual–Intellectual Confrontations of Our Age.* Wentzville, MO: Invictus Books, 2011.

Ruhe, David S. *Door of Hope: The Bahá'í Faith in the Holy Land.* Oxford: George Ronald, 2nd rev. ed. 2001.

Rupp, E. G. *Luther and Erasmus: Free Will and Salvation.* Philadelphia, PA: Westminster Press, 1969.

Sauer, Paul. *The Holy Land Called.: The Story of the Temple Society.* Trans. Gunhild Henley. Bentleigh, VIC: Temple Society Australia, 1991.

Shantz, Douglas H. *An Introduction to German Pietism: Protestant Renewal at the Dawn of the Modern Europe.* Baltimore, Maryland: John Hopkins University Press, 2013.

— *Between Sardis and Philadelphia: The Life and Work of Pietist Court Preacher Conrad Broske.* Leiden and Boston: Brill, 2008.

— (ed.). *A Companion to German Pietism, 1660–1800.* Leiden and Boston: Brill, 2014.

Schneider, Hans. *German Radical Pietism.* Trans. Gerald T. MacDonald. Plymouth: The Scarecrow Press, 2007.

The Spiritual Magazine. Vol. IV (1869). London: James Burns.

Spitz, Lewis W. *The Protestant Reformation 1517–1559: The Rise of Modern Europe.* New York: Harper & Row, 1985.

Stilling, John Henry *The Life of John Henry Stilling.* Trans. E. L. Hazelius. Gettysburg: Theological Seminary, 1831.

Strauss, David Friedrich. *Das Leben Jesu, kritisch bearbeite* (1835). *The Life of Jesus Critically Examined.* Trans. Marian Evans (George Eliot). New York; Calvin Blanchard, 1860. RP New York, Cosimo Classics, 2010.

Taylor, Daniel T. *The Reign of Christ on Earth.* Rev. and ed. H. L. Hastings. Boston: Scriptural Tract Repository, 1882.

Twain, Mark. *The Innocents Abroad or The New Pilgrims' Progress.* Connecticut: American Publishing Company, 1869. RP New York: Signet Classics, 2007.

Vinglas, R. V. *Eschatological Teachings of Luther and Calvin.* Thesis, S.D.A. Theological Seminary, 1948.

Wardin, Albert W. Jr. *On the Edge: Baptists and Other Free Church Evangelicals in Tsarist Russia, 1855–1917.* Eugene, OR: WIPF & Stock, 2013.

Wellcome, Isaac C. *History of the Second Advent Message.* Boston: Advent Christian Publication Society, 1874.

Williamson, George S. *The Longing for a Myth in Germany: Religion and Ascetic Culture from Romanticism to Nietzsche.* Chicago: University of Chicago Press, 2004.

Notes and References

Introduction: A Brief Overview of Christianity in the West

1 The implementation of this new doctrine was alluded to by Isaac C. Wellcome in his book *History of the Second Advent Message* (1874), where he quotes on page 510 from an unspecified document entitled *Church History*: 'from that moment, the distinctive doctrines of the Gospel ceased to be taught generally. The atonement was no longer spoken of; the second advent of Christ and His future Kingdom were denied; the Resurrection of the body was explained away. The conspiracy triumphed under Pope Damascus [A.D. 381], who declared the millennium had already commenced and expelled from the church, as heretics, all who looked for Christ's second Advent and Kingdom.'

2 Coleridge Taylor, quoted in Gilly, *Vigilantius and His Times*, p. 269.

3 Murray, *The Life of John Wycliffe.* p. 29.

4 The Ninety-Five Theses were a turning point not only in Martin Luther's life, but also in the future of the Catholic Church. Luther hoped that by dedicating himself to life as a monk he would acquire the spiritual salvation he longed for, finding inspiration in the writings of St Augustine in his early years and joining the Augustinian monastery in the city of Erfurt; however, his wish for spiritual salvation was unfulfilled, no doubt aided by a visit to Rome in 1510 as a delegate to a church conference, where he was so appalled by what he observed as corruption and immorality amongst the priests, that on his return to Germany he enrolled at the University of Wittenberg in the hope that in studying he would finally find solutions to his spiritual unrest. Not long after having obtained his doctorate and taken up the position of professor of theology at the university, he was preparing a lecture on Paul's Epistle to the Romans, when he was struck by the verse, 'the just will live by faith . . .' (Romans 1:17), and having thought about it for a while, came to the conclusion that salvation didn't come through fear of God or enslavement to religious dogma, but through faith alone. Whilst this was a significant moment for Luther and the Church, the pivotal element leading to major change took place in 1517, when Pope Leo X reaffirmed the use of indulgences in order to finance the building of the new Saint Peter's Basilica. Indulgences offered a way of avoiding punishment for sins and time spent in Purgatory, by giving money and thus providing the Vatican with funds. By the late Middle Ages it had become extremely commercialized and recognized by many as an abuse. When Luther became aware of this

new round of indulgences, he was so incensed that he drew up his Ninety-Five Theses, in which he presented his radical views on the practice of indulgences.

5 The New Testament was published in 1522, the complete Bible in 1534.
6 Calvin, quoted in Taylor, *The Reign of Christ on Earth*, p. 153.
7 Latimer, quoted ibid.
8 Knox, quoted ibid. p. 151.
9 Anabaptist was a term by which many of the new radical reformers soon became known as a result of their strong opinions regarding infant baptism. It was a contentious subject, since for centuries it had been an accepted ritual in the fabric of Christian life, the radicals claiming that since there is no mention of it in the New Testament, it should be reserved for confessing adults who choose to be baptised.

1. Light upon Light: Pietism

1 Borrowed from the title of an introduction to a collection of sermons by Johann Arndt.
2 Shantz, *Between Sardis and Philadelphia: The Life and Work of Pietist Court Preacher Conrad Broske*, p. xxi.
3 The key to naming the society Philadelphia lies in the Biblical Book of Revelation, most specifically Chapters 2 and 3, which are addressed to the seven churches in the Roman province of Asia, one of which was called Philadelphia:

> And to the angel of the church in Philadelphia write; These things saith he that is holy, he that is true, he that hath the key of David, he that openeth, and no man shutteth; and shutteth, and no man openeth (3:7).

> Behold, I come quickly: hold that fast which thou hast, that no man take thy crown. Him that overcometh will I make a pillar in the temple of my God, and he shall go no more out: and I will write upon him the name of my God, and the name of the city of my God, [which is] new Jerusalem, which cometh down out of heaven from my God: and [I will write upon him] my new name (3: 11–13).

> Remember therefore how thou hast received and heard, and hold fast, and repent. If therefore thou shalt not watch, I will come on thee as a thief, and thou shalt not know what hour I will come upon thee (3:3).

4 Berthelsdorf, near the borders of present-day Czech Republic and Poland.

NOTES AND REFERENCES

5 Followers of the first church reformer in the 15th century, Jan Hus. See Introduction.

6 John Wesley (1703–1791) and his brother Charles (1707–1788) led the evangelical revival in the Church of England during the eighteenth century. They attended Oxford University, and due to their strict adherence to guidelines in the Book of Common Prayer regarding worship and discipline, were soon given the label 'Methodists'. In 1735, following ordination, they travelled to the American colony of Georgia, John serving as a missionary and Charles as secretary to Governor Oglethorpe. However, disappointed with the experience, they soon returned to England, where they both underwent a life-changing spiritual conversion; in John's case, it was when he was in the company of some Moravian Brethren and had been deeply affected by reading Martin Luther's Preface to the Epistle to the Romans, as a result of which he become aware of a deep emotional awareness of Christ's love as manifested in freely offered forgiveness of sins and the promise of eternal life. John became a powerful preacher, travelling approximately 8,000 miles a year on horseback, and Charles was known for his writing of over 6,000 hymns. Although the Wesleys' intention was that Methodist Societies should exist within the Anglican Church, they later became a separate church.

7 Mark 13:32: 'about that day or hour no one knows, neither the angels in heaven, nor the Son, but only the Father.' Acts 1:7: 'when they had come together, they asked Him, "Lord, is this the time when you will restore the kingdom to Israel?" Jesus replied, "It is not for you to know the times or periods/seasons that the Father has set by his own authority."'

8 The Book of Ezekiel in the Old Testament of the Bible includes a prophetic vision of the reconstructed Temple in Jerusalem, which itself would become the capital of the Kingdom of God on earth during the promised Messianic age to come.

2. Longing for Heaven': Johann Heinrich Jung-Stilling

1 Jung-Stilling, *The Life of John Henry Stilling*, p. 72.
2 ibid. p. 70.
3 Ratliff, *Pilgrims on the Silk Road*, p. 95.
4 Jung-Stilling, *The Life of John Henry Stilling*, p. 296.
5 ibid. pp. 297–8.
6 Exactly why Jung-Stilling decided to name this place Solyma isn't entirely clear initially, although a cursory investigation does turn up a couple of intriguing possibilities. The first of these comes from *Journal of a Tour in Asia Minor* by William Martin Leake (1824) stating on page 130: 'On the west side of the gulf, a little to the left

of the direction of the route, appeared another range of mountains, (Mount Solyma, then distant about sixty miles) still more lofty than those on the right, and so distant that nothing but the outline was visible'. And in a note: 'there was a pass in Mount Solyma not far from Attalei' (ibid. p. 190). According to these references Solyma existed long before Jung-Stilling wrote his novel.

The second possibility comes from a short passage in the writings of Flavius Josephus, the first-century Romano-Jewish scholar and historian who was born in Jerusalem: 'It was David who first cast the Jebusites out of Jerusalem, and called it by his own name, the city of David; for under our forefather Abraham it was called (Salem or) Solyma; but after that time some say that Homer mentioned it by that name of Solyma (for he named the temple Solyma, according to the Hebrew language, which denotes security)' (*The Works of Flavius Josephus,* vol. 1, Ch. 3). Given the religious context of this passage from Josephus, it's more likely that it was this Solyma which took Jung-Stilling's imagination, and that his interest in reading had at some point taken him to the writings of Josephus as it already had to Homer.

7 Jung-Stilling, *The Life of John Henry Stilling,* p. 298.
8 The Maronite monastery of Our Lady in Canobin (Kannoubeen) lay in the Lebanese mountains; the monks were noted for their cultivation of silkworms, and the economy in that region grew steadily during the 18th century.
9 Jung-Stilling, *The Life of John Henry Stilling,* pp. 304–5.
10 'Melancholy history of German emigrants to Armenia', letter to the editor, in *The Christian Observer,* June 1840, pp. 325–6.
11 *British North American Wesleyan Methodist Magazine* (1842), vol. 2, pp. 182–3.

3. 'The Reign of Christ Will Come, Sire': Baroness Barbara Juliana Von Krüdener

1 'Krüdener, Barbara, Juliana, Baroness von', in *Encyclopaedia Britannica* (1911), vol. 15.
2 ibid.
3 ibid. Visible to the naked eye for 260 days, the comet was known as the 'Great Comet'.
4 'Religious character of the late Emperor Alexander', in *The Christian Observer,* vol. XXX, no. 340 (April 1830), p. 199.
5 Howitt, 'The Baroness Barbara Juliana von Krüdener', in *The Spiritual Magazine,* vol. IV (1 January 1869), pp. 15–16.
6 ibid.
7 'Krüdener, Barbara, Juliana, Baroness von', in *Encyclopaedia Britannica* (1911), vol. 15.

8 'Religious character of the late Emperor Alexander', in *The Christian Observer*, vol. XXX, no. 340 (April 1830), p. 201.

9 ibid. pp. 203–4.

10 'Krüdener, Barbara, Juliana, Baroness von', in *Encyclopaedia Britannica* (1911), vol. 15. Chiliastic belief involves an expectation of the Second Coming of Christ, the establishment of God's Kingdom on earth, and the imminent end of the world.

11 Howitt, 'The Baroness Barbara Juliana von Krüdener', in *The Spiritual Magazine*, vol. IV (1 January 1869), p. 19.

12 ibid. p. 20.

13 'Krüdener, Barbara, Juliana, Baroness von', in *Encyclopaedia Britannica* (1911), vol. 15.

14 This came about as a result of Alexander Ypsilanti's invasion of the Danubian principalities, which opened the Greek War of Independence. Alexander Ypsilanti was a member of a prominent Greek family, a prince of the Danubian Principalities, senior officer of the Imperial Russian cavalry during the Napoleonic Wars, and leader of a secret organization which coordinated the start of the Greek War of Independence against the Ottoman Empire.

4. 'Thy Kingdom Come': Christoph Hoffmann

1 From the Lord's Prayer.

2 Hoffmann, *Jerusalem Journey*, p. 20.

3 ibid. p. 18.

4 ibid. p. 20.

5 ibid. p. 22.

6 ibid. p. 37.

7 Alexander Ypsilanti: see Chapter 3, note 14.

8 Hoffmann, *Jerusalem Journey*, p. 32.

9 ibid. p. 39. As noted in Chapter 1, Johann Albrecht Bengel (1687–1752), born in Württemberg, was a Lutheran Pietist clergyman, mathematician and Greek scholar who was particularly known for his translation of the Greek New Testament. But it was his scholarly study of prophecy which is of interest in the context of Christoph Hoffmann and the community in which he grew up. Bengel's millennial views were peculiarly distinctive, based primarily on the 20th chapter of the Book of Revelation and involving 'a double millennium, viz., a thousand years reign on earth, followed by a thousand years reign in heaven; The first the seventh, the second the eighth years from the creation. The first thousand years beginning, as he thought, in 1836, would be preceded by rapid changes and great judgements (Taylor, *The Reign of Christ on Earth*, p. 243).

Bengel approached his study of the Bible mathematically, and he was fascinated by what he believed to be a definite relationship between dates and time periods passing from the first book in the Bible, Genesis, right through to the Book of Revelation. In an extraordinary, extremely long and Herculean attempt to map out the chronology of the history of the earth from its very beginnings, Bengel came up with the date 18 June 1836 as the day of 'conflict of the Beast out of the Bottomless Pit with the people of God; and his overthrow at the appearance of the Lord'. Bengel then calculated in his Chronological Table that from 1836 to 2836 Satan would be held at bay, followed by another thousand years during which the saints would reign in heaven, with the end of the world, the final judgement, taking place in 3836. Writing in about 1740, he stated:

> The Great Tribulation, which the primitive Church looked for from the future Antichrist, is not arrived, but is very near; for the predictions of the Apocalypse, from the tenth to the fourteenth chapter [Book of Revelation], have been fulfilling for many centuries; and the principal point stands clearer and clearer in view, that within another hundred years, the great expected change of things may take place. Even though within the next five years the Beast's chronological number should still remain unexpired, such a failure in our apocalyptical calculation is no more than the crack of a pane in the window of a large edifice. Still let the remainder stand, especially the great termination which I anticipate for 1836 . . . should the year 1836 pass away without any such remarkable change in public affairs as I have anticipated, some fundamental mistake in the arrangement of my system must be sought after (quoted in Burk, *A Memoir of the Life and Writings of John Albert Bengel*, p. 316).

10 Hoffmann, *Jerusalem Journey*, p. 41.
11 ibid. p. 56.
12 Georg Wilhelm Friedrich Hegel (27 August 1770–14 November 1831) was a prominent figure in German idealism.
13 Hoffmann, *Jerusalem Journey*, p. 63.
14 ibid.
15 ibid. pp. 63–4.
16 ibid. p. 69.
17 ibid. p. 70.
18 ibid.
19 ibid. pp. 70–71.
20 ibid. p. 71.
21 ibid. p. 74.
22 Quoted passages are from an article in the *Review and Herald* of 17

May 1892, written by Pastor L. R. Conradi of Hamburg, Germany, which appear in Loughborough, *The Great Second Advent Movement* (1905), p. 45.

23 Hoffmann, *Jerusalem Journey*, pp. 79–81.
24 ibid. p. 83.
25 ibid. p. 91.
26 ibid. p. 92.
27 Pantheism: the joining of two Greek words, 'pan', meaning all, and 'theism', meaning God. Pantheism is a belief that God is in everything and everything in God.
28 Hoffmann, *Jerusalem Journey*, p. 92.
29 ibid. p. 93.
30 ibid.
31 Hoffmann's interpretation regarding Babylon came from the Book of Revelation, his reading of Chapter 18:4 in particular inspiring his concept of the gathering of God's people in Jerusalem: 'And I heard another voice from heaven, saying, Come out of her, my people, that ye be not partakers of her sins, and that ye receive not of her plagues.' The story of Babylon comes from the Book of Genesis. In Chapter 9:1 God instructs Noah and his family to 'be fruitful, and multiply, and replenish the earth', but they ignored God and gathered at Babel (Mesopotamia) where the rebellious leader, Nimrod, constructed a tower 'lest we be scattered abroad upon the face of the whole earth' (Gen. 11:4). According to the Bible there was only one language at this point, and by building a tower the people wished to demonstrate their own power whilst making sure that they would avoid being dispersed. But the great tower became an object of worship in itself, a veritable stairway to heaven and a powerful force which united the people and turned them away from God. God challenged the people by forcing them to speak in many languages, and to scatter themselves throughout the world, thus breaking their unity and crushing their plans.
32 Hoffmann, *Jerusalem Journey*, pp. 94–5.
33 ibid.

5. Brothers in Arms: Christoph Hoffmann and Georg Hardegg

1 Hoffman, *Jerusalem Journey*, p. 95.
2 ibid.
3 ibid. p. 98. Zerababel was the leader of the first group of Jews – approximately 42,000 – returning from Babylonian captivity. Soon afterwards he laid the foundation for the second Temple in Jerusalem.
4 ibid.
5 ibid. p. 101.

6. 'Gathering of the People of God': No Going Back

1 Hoffmann, *Jerusalem Journey*, p. 101.
2 ibid. p. 102.
3 Still sung by members of the Templer community today.
4 Hoffmann, *Jerusalem Journey*, p. 102.
5 ibid.
6 ibid. p. 103. 'Shocks' are haystacks.
7 ibid. p. 105.
8 ibid. p. 104.
9 ibid. and p. 107.
10 ibid. p. 104.
11 ibid. p. 106.
12 ibid. p. 107.
13 ibid. pp. 107–8.
14 ibid. p. 108.

7. 'Onward and Forward': The Scouting Tour

1 Hoffmann, *Jerusalem Journey*, pp. 108–9.
2 ibid. p. 109.
3 ibid. pp. 111–12.
4 ibid. pp. 112–13.
5 ibid. p. 113.
6 ibid. pp. 113–14.
7 ibid. p. 114.
8 Schneller Orphanage, also known as the Syrian Orphanage, was a German Protestant orphanage operating in Jerusalem from 1860 to 1940, offering education to abandoned and orphaned Arab children. The building was one of the very first to be constructed outside Old Jerusalem.
9 Valentiner was the first spiritual leader of the German Protestant parish which had been established in January 1852.
10 Reference to the Cross in Christian writing, belief and thought is central to the Christian religion, which teaches that Jesus Christ died on the Cross to free man from sin. This is mentioned several times in the New Testament: 'Hereby perceive we the love of God, because he laid down his life for us (I John 3: 16);"For Christ also hath once suffered for sins, the just for the unjust, that he might bring us to God, being put to death in the flesh, but quickened by the Spirit' (I Peter 1:18).
11 Hoffmann, *Jerusalem Journey*, p. 115.
12 ibid. pp. 117–19.
13 ibid. pp. 123–4.
14 ibid. p. 125.

15 ibid. p. 126.
16 ibid.
17 ibid. pp. 126–7.
18 ibid. p. 127.

8. 'The Times Spoken Of in All the Prophecies': Facing the Challenge

1 The Second Italian War of Independence, also known as the Franco-Austrian War, Austro-Sardinian War and the Italian War, was fought by the French Empire and the Kingdom of Sardinia against the Austrian Empire; it began in the spring of 1859, encouraging conjecture amongst the Templer leaders concerning the coming of the apocalypse. This involved speculation that Napoleon III was the 'beast' that comes up from the bottomless pit (Rev. 11:7), and calculations regarding the appearance of the Antichrist and the Second Coming of Christ. Indeed, Christoph Paulus wrote a paper, *Insights into the Prophecies of St. John's Revelation*, in which he predicted this event. Hardegg didn't feel that precise timing was essential, and Christoph Hoffmann focused on the critical matter of bringing God's people together.

2 As King, he was the 'sovereign and highest bishop in the State' on whom 'rested the responsibility for public welfare' (Sauer, *The Holy Land Called*, p. 35).

3 Hoffmann, *Mein Weg nach Jerusalem* (1884), p. 467, as translated in Sauer, *The Holy Land Called*, p. 36.

4 Hoffmann, *Jerusalem Journey*, p. 129.

5 ibid. pp. 129–30.

6 ibid. p. 108.

7 Christians waiting for the return of Christ studied the prophecies of both the Old and New Testaments for clues; from reading Luke 21: 24 and 27 they believed that Christ would return after the return of the Jews to the Holy Land, following their period of banishment. Luke states: 'And they shall fall by the edge of the sword, and shall be led away captive into all nations: and Jerusalem shall be trodden down of the Gentiles, until the times of the Gentiles be fulfilled . . . And then shall they see the Son of man coming in a cloud with power and great glory.'
   George Jones Adams, born in New Jersey in 1811, was a failed Shakespearean actor, merchant tailor and trained Methodist minister, becoming a member of the church of the Latter Day Saints (LDS) in 1840, the leader, Joseph Smith, appointing him as an apostle to Russia in readiness for the Mormon political kingdom. Following Joseph Smith's death in 1844 Adams created havoc when he claimed to be the 'Thirteenth Apostle' therefore not only believing himself to be of greater importance than the Apostle Paul, but also above the authority

of the Quorum of the Twelve Apostles, a governing body of the LDS church, which promptly had him excommunicated. Involvement with a break-off denomination of the church led by James Strang resulted in Adams crowning Strang as the spiritual king of Israel with a metal crown, and being appointed as his leader before being excommunicated for drunkenness, adultery and misappropriation of funds.

By 1860 Adams had created his own church in New England, calling it the Church of Messiah and appointing himself as a prophet of Christ to the world. Five years later he decided to set out for Palestine with some of his followers in order to prepare it for the return of the Jews in order to precipitate the expected Second Coming of Jesus. Before setting out he changed his name to George Washington Joshua Adams, thus connecting himself to George Washington in the United States and Joshua of the Old Testament, both of whom were recognized as successful builders of nations/countries. Such was the enthusiasm of his followers that they donated most of their funds to the project. Having travelled to Palestine in order to set up the purchase of some land near Jaffa, his first mission on returning home was to advance an agreement through the US President and Secretary of State, guaranteeing that the government of the Ottoman Empire would respect the land sale.

The 156 members of the Church of the Messiah duly landed in Jaffa at the end of September 1866, bringing with them farming tools, sacks of seed potatoes, and building materials for erecting 22 houses, and initially setting up camp on the beach and accepting food and water from the local Arabs. Despite extremely difficult conditions and the loss of nine lives within the first few weeks, the pilgrims managed to set up a colony just outside Jaffa, naming it Adams City. However, their crops were stolen and starvation beckoned, added to which erratic treatment by the Ottoman authorities made life insecure, all of which tempted many pilgrims to return home. When Adams withheld the funds they had given him for the project, a missionary at the Protestant mission bought the land from five pilgrim families, thus enabling them to pay for their passage back to America. In the meantime Adams, who had taken refuge in the bottle, seemed unable to control the situation, with the American consul to the Ottoman Empire taking on the responsibility for assuring 26 settlers a safe passage.

By December 1867 those remaining in Jaffa had completely run out of funds and food, at which point all but 20 of the original pilgrims left for home on a boat named the *Quaker City*; one of their fellow passengers happened to be the writer Mark Twain, who left a memorable description of his impressions on the voyage:

At Jaffa we had taken on board some forty members of a very celebrated community. They were male and female; babies, young boys and young girls; young married people, and some who had passed a shade beyond the prime of life. I refer to the 'Adams Jaffa Colony'. Others had deserted before. We left in Jaffa Mr. Adams, his wife, and fifteen unfortunates who not only had no money but did not know where to turn or whither to go. Such was the statement made to us. Our forty were miserable enough in the first place, and they lay about the decks seasick all the voyage, which about completed their misery, I take it. However, one or two young men remained upright, and by constant persecution we wormed out of them some little information. They gave it reluctantly and in a very fragmentary condition, for, having been shamefully humbugged by their prophet, they felt humiliated and unhappy. In such circumstances people do not like to talk.

Adams and his wife sailed for England a year later, and those who remained eventually sold their property to a group of settlers called the German Templers. Adams himself made a second, failed attempt, to settle Palestine, and when confronted by his past activities, denied any involvement at all. He set up another Church of the Messiah in Philadelphia, and died of typhoid complications in 1880. The Americans sold most of their land to a Christian Mission in Jaffa (*Innocents Abroad or The New Pilgrims' Progress*, Ch, LVII, p. 613).
8 Hoffmann, *Jerusalem Journey*, p. 130.
9 ibid.

9. 'Gratitude and hope': Fulfilling the dream

1 The Iron Gate of Turkey is a gorge on the river Danube, and forms part of the border between Romania and Serbia.
2 Hoffmann, *Jerusalem Journey*, pp. 132–3.
3 ibid. p. 133.
4 ibid. p. 134. See Chapter 10 for further about the Reverend Huber.
5 ibid.
6 Consul-General Weber in Beirut.
7 Hoffmann, *Jerusalem Journey*, p. 136.
8 ibid. p. 137.
9 Twain, *The Innocents Abroad*, pp. 473–4.
10 Hoffmann, *Jerusalem Journey*, p. 138. See also Mark Twain's description of these Templers in Chapter 8 above, note 7.

10. 'Could the Signs of the Times be Clearer?': A Meeting of Minds

1 A four-wheeled vehicle drawn by horses.

2 Quoted in Momen, *The Bábí and Bahá'í Religions 1844–1944: Some Contemporary Western Accounts*, p. 236.

3 Quoted ibid. p. 237. It's probable that the Bahá'ís he met were Khalil Mansur and his brother, Aqa 'Abdullah, who had recently travelled from exile in Mosul, Iraq, and had set themselves up as copper-smiths in Haifa. Khalil took care of pilgrims arriving in Haifa on their way to Akka, where they hoped to be able to see Bahá'u'lláh, and Khalil regularly visited Akka where he sold his copper, collected letters which he posted from Haifa, and gave reports on how the pilgrims were faring.

4 The Lawḥ-i-Hirtik, see Appendix for translation by Lambden.

5 Quoted in Momen, *The Bábí and Bahá'í Religions*, p. 218. This interview probably took place in the House of 'Údí Khammár.

6 Tablet to Ḥájí Mírzá Ḥaydar-'Ali of Isfahan, quoted in Lambden, 'A Tablet of Bahá'-Alláh to Georg David Hardegg, the Lawḥ-i Hartík', at https://hurqalya.ucmerced.edu/node/237/.

7 Bahá'u'lláh, *Gleanings from the Writings of Bahá'u'lláh*, XIV, p. 31.

8 ibid. X, pp. 12–13.

9 Bahá'u'lláh, Lawḥ-i-Aqdas (The Most Holy Tablet, also known as the Tablet to the Christians), in *Bahá'u'lláh, Tablets of Bahá'u'lláh Revealed after the Kitáb-i-Aqdas*, p. 11.

10 He was also US consular agent for Haifa.

11. 'These Doors Shall Be Opened': An Uncertain Future

1 The other houses were in Jerusalem, with 25, Sarona 41, and Jaffa 33. There were also commercial buildings in Jerusalem, Jaffa and Sarona, having 25, 15 and 41 respectively.

2 The architect was Dr. Ing. Gottlieb Schumacher, and the builders Christian and Fritz Beilharz.

3 Quoted in Esslemont, *Bahá'u'lláh and the New Era*, p. 34.

4 The house was called Bayt-i-Fanduq.

5 Laurence Oliphant (1829–1888) was a British diplomat whose deep religious faith inspired him to develop, around 1878–79, a plan for Jewish colonization in Palestine in fulfilment of Christian prophecies regarding the 'end times'. Welcomed by Turkish ministers in the Ottoman Empire and also in England, it was nevertheless rejected by the Sultan, who was mistrustful of British intentions.

6 Henderson, *The Life of Laurence Oliphant*, p. 229.

7 This was a house on a corner of Allenby Road which belonged to the Templer Elyas Abyad.

8 This Templer house stands opposite Me'ir Rutberg Street where it meets Hagefen Street. The inscription is now over a window.

9 Ruhe, *Door of Hope*, p. 229, note 5.

10 For further information on the Báb, for this incident and what followed see for example Day, *Journey to a Mountain.*

11 Cornelia Wortz, unpublished recollections in Bahá'í World Centre Library, recounted in Day, *Journey to a Mountain,* p. 113.

12 Knight of the Most Excellent Order of the British Empire.

13 Bahá'u'lláh, Tablet of Carmel, in Bahá'u'lláh, *Gleanings from the Writings of Bahá'u'lláh,* XI, pp. 15–16.

Epilogue

1 In January 1919 the Pan-German nationalist and anti-Semitic German Workers' Party was founded in Germany, renamed the National Socialist German Workers' Party (NSDAP) when Adolf Hitler took control of the organization in the early 1920s.

2 From *The Sentinel,* 1933.

3 On this night, in cities all over Germany, Jewish shop windows were broken, homes destroyed, and synagogues set alight. Jewish citizens suffered beatings, arrest, and even in some cases, death, at the hands of marauding Nazi sympathizers.

4 By 1948 the Zionist colonists and Palestinian Arabs were battling for Palestine, the Haganah attacking Palestinian villages, members of the irregular Arab forces attacking Jewish neighbourhoods from across the borders, and members of both sides firing at the police and troops who were attempting to keep the situation in check. British Mandatory forces were caught in the middle as preparations were being put in place for their evacuation via the port at Haifa in April 1948. By the beginning of May approximately 175,000 Palestinians had already fled Palestine, and two weeks later, on 14 May, Israel declared independence.

Lawḥ-i Hartik

1 Lambden, 'Some notes and commentary on the Lawh-i Hartik, Part Two'.

Index

About the author

Carolyn Sparey Fox is a professional musician based in the United Kingdom. She won a scholarship to study at the Royal Academy of Music in London, and was latterly principal viola with the BBC Scottish Symphony Orchestra. She is also a commissioned composer. Amongst musicians she has collaborated with are violinist Sir Yehudi Menuhin and conductor Sir Simon Rattle, and she performed in the first London production of *Jesus Christ Superstar*.

As a result of her first book, *The Half of It was Never Told*, she was invited by the creators of the drama-documentary film, *The Gate*, which tells the story of the dawn of the Bahá'í Faith, to appear in the film as an expert on 19th-century Adventism.

www.ingramcontent.com/pod-product-compliance
Lightning Source LLC
Chambersburg PA
CBHW070807100426
42742CB00012B/2277